A Front Row Seat at the War

An Airman's Experiences
as a B-17 Bombardier with the 390th Bomb Group
during World War II

Lt. Arthur W. Ordel, Jr.

Printed in the United States of America

Cover photo, bottom:
This is the view from the bombardier's station of a World War II–era B-17 bomber after it took off from Crites Field in Waukesha. The historic plane was part of Wings Over Waukesha air show.
Image credit: Peter Zuzga, Waukeshanow.com

First Edition
© 2015 Arthur Ordel, Jr.
ISBN: 978-1-938205-18-7
Library of Congress Control Number: 2015936411

BLACKWELL
PRESS
LYNCHBURG, VIRGINIA

BLACKWELLPRESS.NET

To my brother,
Torpedoman Robert Fred Ordel,
and all the others missing in action
and killed in action,
and were unable to write their own stories.

Bombardier's Position

1st Lt. Arthur Ordel flew 35 missions as a bombardier with the
570th Squadron, 390th Bomb Group, 8th Air Force.
He was awarded the Distinguished Flying Cross
and Air Medal with four oak leaf clusters

CONTENTS

Prologue

I have been asked many times how I decided to write about my experiences in World War II.

My career as a professional forester with several different large corporations ended in 1989 when I retired from "woods work". On my 75th birthday Grace was still working at the University of Virginia and Angie attended "WorkSource" daily, and I was at home alone. I could not stand soap operas, and so I began to write a few paragraphs about the 36 months I had spent in the US Army back in the '40s.

In 1983 I had met up again with co-pilot Chuck Baker and navigator Bob Munroe at a 390th Group Reunion in Dayton, Ohio. I learned they had both kept personal war time diaries of our crew's life together. With a copy of these and the anthology of the 390th Bomb Group, I began to write seriously, but secretly! After I had finished writing, I put the pages away in my foot locker and let it all simmer for a few years.

I eventually resurrected all this, and showed it to Grace. I asked her what she thought, and she said "We'll make it into a book." That is the brief story of how this book came into being over these many years.

Acknowledgements

It is our pleasure to note names of the following persons who have so willingly helped with this book from the first page.
Charles N. Baker
Margaret Duncan
Steve Gilmore
Cindy Ordel Lemmons
Alexandra Ordel
Bill Ordel III
David Ward Ordel
Julia Vickers

Grace H. Ordel   *Art Ordel Jr*

World War II
On The Horizon

CHAPTER 1

One Step Ahead of the Draft Board

Covington, Virginia

1939 May

I graduated from high school in Covington, Virginia, on May 22, 1939 (my eighteenth birthday). The United States and the whole world had been in a severe economic depression for ten years, however things were finally brightening.

I badly wanted to go to college, but being the oldest of five children I realized the money was just not available.

Employment in Covington was still hard to come by and so the summer of 1939 I took various low paying jobs. The main one was on the soda fountain in a local pharmacy. The pay was ten cents an hour, plus all the ice cream I could eat.

Over Labor Day 1939, my Boy Scout troop went on a camping trip to Neola, West Virginia, in the Monongahela National Forest. I enjoyed my scouting experiences immensely and had earned Eagle Scout rank the previous summer. Along with our scoutmaster Harvey Shepherd, we left on a Saturday morning for a two-day trip. Harvey was a chemist with West Virginia Pulp & Paper Co. known locally as Westvaco. He had graduated from Virginia Polytechnic Institute (Virginia Tech) and held a reserve commission of 1st lieutenant in the US Army Chemical Warfare Branch.

1938 Summer, Art as an Eagle Scout at Camp Shenandoah in Virginia

Ordel family in 1937 - Art, Bob; Mother and Dad; Ron, Jessie and Ralph

On Monday morning Harvey drove down to Neola Village for supplies and when he returned I noticed he had an extremely odd expression on his face. I asked if something had happened in town; it was then he told me the news. Germany had invaded Poland the previous day and it appeared that war had broken out in Europe. I replied "How could such an event so far away ever affect us?" Within a few months Harvey was called to active duty and six years later he was a full colonel in the United States Army.

1939 October my life definitely took an upswing when I was fortunate to be hired by Westvaco at their Covington paper mill. The salary was a magnificent forty-five and one-half cents an hour. The work turned out to be very hard and tiring, but I fully realized this would become my ticket to college.

At work I was assigned to "shifts" which meant working from 7:00 a.m.-3:00 p.m. one week, 3:00 p.m.-11:00 p.m. the second week, and 11:00 p.m.-7:00 a.m. the third week, then

"How could such an event so far away ever affect us?"

The Gordon Chappell Orchestra, Clifton Forge and Covington, VA shown on New Year's Eve 1939. Art, age 18 and 3rd from the left, back row.

back to 7:00 a.m.-3:00 p.m. There were no meal breaks, and employees ate while working whenever there was a spare minute. I never became acclimated to shift work, and my system never knew when it was time to eat or to sleep. I worked in the finishing room where one-ton and two-ton rolls of warm paper from the paper making-machine were re-wound into smaller rolls. The smaller rolls were trimmed and wrapped for shipping. An overhead crane moved the heaviest rolls, but the smaller rolls, weighing several hundred pounds, were pushed on hand dollies. Forklifts had not yet been provided. I weighed only 135 pounds that fall and I moved the rolls of paper with some difficulty.

In the autumn of my senior year of high school my parents had purchased a $40.00 second-hand trombone for me. I played in the Covington High School Band for a year and by graduation my performance was passable and enabled me to join the local "big band" known as "Gordon Chappell."

I played with this group two or three nights a month, earning $5.00 for each four-hour session. This money was added to my paper-mill earnings and since I was very frugal, by August 1940 I had salted away $600, which was enough for one year of college, plus the money required to purchase my military school uniforms.

VIRGINIA TECH

In August 1940 I enrolled in Virginia Polytechnic Institute, Blacksburg, VA. I was the first Ordel to ever attend college and my parents were very proud of me.

I did not own a trunk, so my father went to the local lumber yard and had a large wooden

The honor system was so ingrained at Tech and for that reason I could safely leave all my worldly possessions overnight on the steps of that very public building.

box made for me to keep my possessions safe. Then my parents drove me to Blacksburg, along with my three younger siblings and the big box. Upon arrival, having no idea what to do next, they unloaded me and the big box on the steps of the Student Activities Building (SAB) and drove away on the return trip to Covington.

I struck up a conversation with a couple of other new students who said they had found a room for the night and were headed downtown to "check out things." I left my big box on the steps for the night and joined these guys. Next day I found my assigned room, and my roommate was a school friend from Covington. With the help of several other students we moved my box to the safety of my new dorm room. The honor system was so ingrained at Tech and for that reason I could safely leave all my worldly possessions overnight on the steps of that very public building.

In 1940 Tech was a land-grant full-time military college, one of seven in the US, and the student enrollment was entirely male. We arose to the sound of "Reveille" and went to bed at "Taps." The dorms were the "barracks" and the dining hall was the "mess hall." We were issued Springfield 30-06 rifles, relics of World War I, and wore uniforms full time. In the freshman year, students were known as "rats" and were constantly hazed by the sophomores. The most visible were two Jewish students who had been really tormented by

1940 Art as a VPI Freshman in formal mess jacket photo. (Credit 1940 VPI yearbook, The Bugle)

sophomores the previous year. They had been forced to give Nazi salutes and say "Heil Hitler" to upperclassmen. This resulted in frustrations which were taken out on our "rat" class. There was no recourse and looking back, I do not know how I endured the constant harassment, but thankfully I did. I continued my musical sideline by joining the Tech marching band, the famous "Highty Tighties."

My parents wrote to me every week and enclosed a one dollar bill in each letter. This was the only spending money I had while in those first two years of college.

I signed up for ROTC (Reserve Officer Training Corps) and was assigned to the Coast Artillery Branch where I learned that our coastal guns were capable of shooting twelve miles out into the Atlantic ocean. With this knowledge I felt really safe and secure, and thought "Nobody is gonna mess with us."

College life took all my time and I am sure that very few of my classmates gave any thought to what was happening across either ocean. I do recall viewing a movie produced by the Germans called *Victory In The West*. It was a propaganda film showing the rapid conquest Blitzkrieg (lightning war) of Holland, Belgium, and France. I found this picture very impressive.

Sometime in 1940 the US Congress passed the "draft" (Selective Service Act) which required all able-bodied males to serve one year in the military. This law was highly unpopular with most Tech students as we were mostly unable to accept the idea of our country being in imminent danger.

I returned to paper mill-work the summer of 1941. This time I was given a much better job with all daylight work, less heavy lifting, and an increase in pay rate to sixty cents an hour. I also had expected to return to my musical career to earn extra money, but I soon found the orchestra had been disbanded since several of the key performers had been drafted.

Late August found me back at Tech and without the burden of the "rat" system. I was able to settle into academia and again gave little thought to events in Europe.

07 December 1941 was a quiet Sunday afternoon in the dorms, when suddenly, without warning, everything changed, as student radios blared reports of a Japanese "sneak attack" on US military installations at Pearl Harbor, Hawaii. Bedlam erupted. No one could believe it, how could these inferior monkeys do this to our mighty United States?

We cadets marched up and down the dorm halls singing "Goodbye Mamma, I'm off to Yokohama and on to Tokyo." Senior cadets brandished their ceremonial sabers and lower classmen waved the old Springfield rifles. It was fortunate that we had no ammo available for those rifles.

The following day Congress declared war on Japan. A day or two later Hitler declared war on the US. It did not take long for me and my fellow students to realize our situation. We were officially in the ROTC (Reserve Officer Training Corps) and also were the optimum age for military service. In the meantime Congress amended the draft from one year to "the duration plus six months."

In January 1942 my oldest brother, Bob, enlisted in the Navy and was sent to boot camp in Norfolk, Virginia. Bob was nineteen years old and had been living with relatives in Pennsylvania, working as a machinist. Following boot camp training, the Navy sent him to machinist school and upon graduation he received the rating of Torpedoman 3rd class.

In March 1942 I received "Greetings" from the draft board ordering me to report for

I decided if I were to fight a war, I did not want to be toting a rifle. I would much prefer to fight a war seated.

duty. I had been in military school just long enough to hate a rifle with passion. The Springfield, a relic of "the war to end all wars," weighed about nine pounds and had to be kept scrupulously clean without one speck of dust. I decided if I were to fight a war, I did not want to be toting a rifle. I would much prefer to fight a war seated.

My attention was drawn to the many posters around campus touting the advantages of flying with the Army Air Corps. "Be a Commissioned Officer," "Wild Blue Yonder," "Sit Down in an Airplane," and "Get Those Silver Wings." These slogans all appealed to me. The audacious raid led by Jimmy Doolittle on Tokyo, from the aircraft carrier *Hornet*, hit the newspapers and radios. I thought this sounded pretty neat, so I decided to become a bomber pilot, and promptly applied for Aviation Cadet Training (ACT).

Early one morning around the end of April, I boarded an army bus with about three dozen other Techmen and journeyed to Roanoke, Virginia, to take the ACT entrance exam. Written testing began at 8:00 a.m. and lasted four hours. At noon the officer-in-charge said,

"You are underweight and you have low blood pressure, but the army will take care of the first and low is better than high." I just could not believe my good luck in being accepted.

"pencils down," and we were told to go for something to eat and to return at 1:00 p.m. Upon returning they announced that six men had passed the first part of the test and would begin physical examinations immediately. I was one of the six remaining applicants who spent the following three hours being poked, prodded, and suffering many indignities. When finally they announced that two had passed the physical tests, I could hardly believe it. Out of three dozen college students, mostly seniors, only two had been accepted as aviation cadets and I was one. I asked the doctor if he had any comments on my health. He replied, "You are underweight and you have low blood pressure, but the army will take care of the first and low is better than high." I just could not believe my good luck in being accepted.

It was a subdued bunch returning to Blacksburg that evening, except for the two of us who had passed. We rode back quietly on cloud nine.

Before we left Roanoke I requested a deferment until June 1st in order to complete my sophomore year. They agreed and I was handed a stack of papers, including one for my parents' signatures of permission to allow me to fly. I didn't think they would sign for me because my brother Bob was now a Navy torpedoman, and they would not want two of us on dangerous duty. The army officer then updated the form to 22 May, 1942, my 21st birthday, and I was "signed up." He said the draft board would be notified that I now belonged to the Army Air Corps and on my birthday, sure enough, I received a confirming letter.

I had expected to be called to active duty immediately but the call took four and a half months to arrive. After a restless, aimless summer at home in Covington, I finally received notice to report on 02 October, 1942.

IN THE ARMY NOW

No doubt it was traumatic for my parents, but I was itching and ready to "get going." 02 October, some two dozen fledgling aviation cadets gathered in Roanoke for additional processing. That evening we were invited by a men's civic club (probably Rotary) to have dinner with them at the Hotel Patrick Henry. After dinner we were taken to the train station, put aboard and informed that our destination was Nashville, Tennessee.

On the train I was assigned an upper berth and enjoyed a night of good sound sleep. I awoke the next morning ready for a fine breakfast. I cannot remember what I ate, but when the check arrived I was horrified to see I had spent eighty-five cents. Never in my life had I blown so much money on one breakfast.

The day passed quickly, as I enjoyed sitting by the window watching all the unfamiliar scenery. As we went through Chattanooga I began to feel a bit unsettled for never had I been so far away from family and home. The train was five cars long and filled with future aviation cadets, mostly from New York and Washington, D.C.

Twenty hours later the train pulled into a rail siding on the Nashville Army Classification Center. It was a very dark night and a drizzling rain was falling.

CHAPTER 2

The Army Classification Center

Nashville, Tennessee

1942 October

We arrived at the Nashville Army Air Base after dark in a drizzling rain. This base served as the classification center for the US Army Air Corps Training Command east of the Mississippi River. An aviation cadet would pass through here taking a multitude of specialized tests, which would determine his future in the military.

I embarked upon my army experience with almost $20 in my pocket. My material possessions were the civilian clothes on my back, and back in Virginia a set of used Virginia Tech uniforms, schoolbooks, and my second hand trombone. I owed the state of Virginia $150.00, which I had borrowed to complete my second year of college. My personal balance sheet was definitely in the red.

Arriving in Nashville, my initial reaction to army life was positive. Leaving the train we were marched to the mess hall, where we were served a surprisingly good meal with as much as we wanted to eat. It surely beat college food.

After the meal, we gathered our luggage and marched to the barracks which looked as if they had been built the day before. These were constructed of rough lumber with no sign of paint on the boards which were so green; one could almost see squirrel tracks. There was an unlit coal stove in the middle of the building, and a latrine at one end. The room contained fifty cots, closely spaced, but no other furniture.

Shortly we were ordered to "fall in" and we marched about a mile, still in the easy rain, to a boxcar on a railroad siding. It contained mattresses and we each took one and marched back to our barracks. We then returned to another boxcar and were issued two wool GI blankets and a pillow. Once back at the barracks we removed our soggy clothes and lay down on soggy beds, with no sheets or pillow cases. We were very tired and soon settled down to a night of soggy sleep. My second reaction to army life was negative.

The next day we marched three times to meals, but we were otherwise not allowed away from the immediate area of our barracks. We were told this was a temporary location for us and that we might move at a moment's notice. The day was spent getting acquainted with classmates and conjecturing about our futures. On the second day a corporal came by and told us we would be here several more days. Also if we wished, he could get us (purchase) some balls, mitts, horseshoes, and other athletic gear, to help pass the time. Most of us chipped in a dollar and handed him the money. The next morning right after breakfast, we were told to pack our bags. We were going for physical exams, would be receiving uniforms, and would not be returning to this site. We never again saw the corporal, any athletic gear, or our money. Arriving at the new location, we were each given a cardboard box, told to remove all civilian clothes, pack them in the box, and address it to our hometown. All we were allowed to keep were our toilet articles.

So there we were, several hundred potential "officers and gentlemen," naked as jaybirds each holding a comb, a toothbrush, and a razor. We started down the lines of doctors and other medical personnel who would be examining us. At the first station, we received a shot in each arm. The rumor was that a person got the tetanus shots first because the typhoid needle was rusty. That was the most complete physical I have ever had. I cannot think of a thing they missed. It took all morning to complete this process.

Several of the guys in our group did not pass this exam, and were eliminated from the Aviation Cadet Training Program before they even began pre-flight school. Since they were still in the US Army, they were sent on to other schools such as gunnery, radio, or mechanics.

Still in our "birthday suits," we crossed the hall to the supply room and began receiving uniforms. We were issued the works: starting out with socks, underwear, shoes, shirts, pants, belt, necktie, fatigues, blouse, field jacket, an overcoat, hat, and all the insignia that had to be pinned or sewn on. We also each received two large barracks bags to pack everything in. We had arrived at the medical building in civilian clothing and exited looking like the rookies we were, smelling to high heaven of moth balls. Last but certainly not least, I received my pair of "dog-tags" with my serial number 3062784. This number would follow me every step of my cadet life and would be on every paper or document along with my name.

From the medical building, we straggled along. We carried our loaded bags to a different barracks and staked out a bed by throwing the bags on it. Again, we marched to a railroad car for a new mattress, blankets, pillow, and GLORY BE, two sheets, and a pillowcase. Fortunately, the rain had stopped and all the bedding was dry. These barracks were similar to the last ones, new, rough, unpainted wood, but heated with two coal stoves. The building was two stories and housed a hundred cadets. The latrine was a nearby building, which meant one had to take a walk to use it. I would guess it had a hundred basins and large open showers with a dozen sprays in each. There must have been at least fifty commodes installed about six inches apart with no partitions between. Cadets, like privates, had absolutely no privacy. Since this building served several barracks, the morning rush hour was a sight to behold. Day or night, the latrine was always crowded.

My first night to sleep in my new barracks didn't occur until the second night, since I was posted for guard duty. This duty lasted twenty-four hours that was broken into shifts of four hours on and four hours off. My post was a stretch of fence out in the boondocks, on the perimeter of the base. I was armed with a billy club and a flashlight, transported to the area in a jeep, which dropped me off and then disappeared into the night. As I walked this lonely beat I wondered, what I would do if a NAZI saboteur came over the fence and stuck a gun to my nose. I had received a shot in each arm that morning, and both arms were paralyzed. I could not move my arms enough to remove the brand new GI overcoat, issued that morning. I kept my coat on during my four hours off. Fortunately, for national security, all the bad guys were still across the ocean.

Next morning everyone was marched to the athletic field. I had never deliberately exercised a day in my life. Now I realized that aching muscles would be a part of my routine each day. Once again, serious reservations about Army life were beginning to invade my thoughts. Almost every afternoon we were put through some sort of ordeal: physical or psychological. These tests would determine which further training we would undergo to become either a pilot, navigator, bombardier, or an officer with some other "ground" specialty. At any point in the classification process, a cadet could be eliminated from the Aviation Cadet Training Program and assigned to a different Army Air Corps school. Of course, every man among us dreamed of becoming a pilot, for they were considered the glamour boys of all the services.

Much class time was spent in lectures on a variety of military topics. We were taught military law, Articles of War, discipline, first aid, and how to behave as an officer and gentleman. All of this was interspersed with marching and drilling. We were kept very busy and had no time to even think.

My first time off the base, I took a fifteen-cent bus ride into Nashville, and as I got off the bus, I was handed a coupon for a one-dollar portrait at a nearby photo shop. I took advantage of this offer and had my first picture in uniform made and mailed home.

The rain was drizzling and all I could see were more uniforms. I decided to go to a movie and when the lights came on at the end of the picture I noticed that no one was sitting near me. My soggy new uniform reeked of moth balls and everyone had moved away from me.

I enjoyed my stay at Nashville, but my main memory of that base is rain, mud, and cold. We marched in an Armistice Day parade in downtown Nashville on November 11. All I can recall is how miserably cold we were. Shortly after our class left Nashville, an influenza epidemic broke out and the base was quarantined for several weeks.

At the end of my time at the classification center, I was notified I had qualified for pilot school, and would be attending pre-flight school at Maxwell Field, Alabama. I was ecstatic to say the least, and had no doubt that I would become a renowned ace.

On our next to last night at Nashville, we decided that we would sleep late the next morning and skip all scheduled events. Next morning, a Saturday, at ten o'clock a major happened to walk by and saw the night light still burning on the entrance stoop. He came in and was astounded to see everyone still in bed. In a very chilly tone, he told us to think about getting out of bed and in a big hurry. Later the same day, right after our evening meal, the major returned, accompanied by two sergeants. He announced there had been a change of plans and ordered us to return all bedding to supply at once. Once we had done so, he informed us that we would be under the supervision of the sergeants who would march us

around the base until time for the train to leave the next morning. We marched all night. Following an early breakfast we picked up our bags and marched to the railroad siding. It was one weary bunch of cadets that climbed aboard the train that Sunday morning.

I cannot remember the ride to Montgomery, Alabama. I must have slept the whole trip.

1942 October. Cadet Arthur Ordel in his first photo in uniform. Used coupon to have photo taken for $1.

Training
to Serve

CHAPTER 3

Pre-Flight Pilot School

Montgomery, Alabama
1942 November

We arrived at Maxwell Field (an old military base) in the afternoon. We were immediately pleased with the living quarters. No rough unpainted lumber, instead we found permanent brick buildings. The roads were paved and the grass lawns were mowed, no mud anywhere. Cadets were assigned six to a room with three double-deck beds, a desk, and a bathroom between each two rooms. We were a bit crowded but had a couple of chairs and a closet. In peacetime only two men would have occupied this room, but in 1942 we were at war.

The mess hall was another matter. Of all the places I was stationed during military life, the food served here was the worst. The Army allowed sixty-six cents a day to feed an enlisted man, but allowed $1.00 a day for an aviation cadet. I have always wondered if that mess officer became wealthy stealing from the cadet program.

Bright and early on Monday morning, we began instruction. The classes included aerodynamics, meteorology, air craft identification, Morse Code, and the internal combustion engine. Physical training continued, but with one addition: three days a week, a run of the seven-mile perimeter of the base. This was done in formation with no lagging or falling out allowed. Strangely enough, I eventually came to enjoy this activity. The other three days we continued calisthenics, but I never grew to like those. The ground school was interesting, and not difficult. I began to feel that I was now in the Air Corps, not just in the army.

We were issued gas masks for a training exercise. We were taken out to a field where a large room-size tent had been set up and filled with poison gas. Putting on the masks, we were invited to enter. We walked from one end of the tent to the other end and as we came out, we were told to remove the mask in order to get a good whiff of the gas.

Another day we were introduced to the high-altitude chamber. This heavy metal cylinder resembled a submarine with small portholes, and one larger hole which was the entrance to the tank. This device held seven cadets and one instructor. We put on oxygen masks. The door was bolted shut and a pump started reducing the pressure. This served to simulate flying at high altitude where the lack of oxygen and pressure do not sustain life. One cadet volunteered to be the guinea pig and he would not wear his mask while the pressure was being reduced. He was given pencil and paper to write answers to the simple questions the instructor asked. As the pressure went down, his writing became worse and eventually was illegible. Somewhere between 18,000 and 20,000 feet he passed out and the instructor immediately replaced his oxygen mask. In a minute or so he awakened with no ill effects. This experience demonstrated the importance of wearing oxygen masks at the altitudes we would be flying. We learned the "friendly skies" were frequently quite unfriendly.

One day I caught some kind of bug, and was feeling very unwell. I went on sick call and joined a long line of other "sickies." When my turn came the doctor took a quick look at me, wrote some numbers on a piece of paper, and instructed me to give it to the sergeant down the hall. The sergeant read it and handed me an envelope containing a handful of pills with instructions. He then produced a tumbler filled with castor oil and told me to drink quickly because he needed the glass for the next person. He advised me that if I needed water there was a water fountain at the far end of the hall.

He was given pencil and paper to write answers to the simple questions the instructor asked. As the pressure went down, his writing became worse and eventually was illegible. Somewhere between 18,000 and 20,000 feet he passed out.

I spent the rest of the day in my room and later, when my roommates returned, one of them said he had something to cure me. He got a bottled Coke, poured half of it out, refilled it with whiskey he had snuck in, and told me to drink. I took one gulp, laid down and swore to myself that never again would I go to an army doctor. I also swore to be a teetotaler from that day forward.

Another training day was spent on the shooting range, where we fired the 30-06 Springfield rifle which I had hated so much at Virginia Tech. We also fired the carbine (a neat little rifle), the .45 automatic pistol, the Thompson sub-machine gun, and a water-cooled .30-caliber machine gun.

SOUTHEAST ARMY AIR FORCES TRAINING CENTER

ARMY AIR FORCES PRE-FLIGHT SCHOOL (PILOT)

Upon the recommendation of his Tactical Officer I do hereby appoint

Aviation Cadet ORDEL, A. W. , a Corporal in the ARMY AIR FORCES PRE-FLIGHT SCHOOL (PILOT) to rank as such from the Second day of January 19 43 He is therefore carefully and diligently to discharge his duties as Corporal , and all cadets coming under his command are strictly charged and required to be obedient to his orders as such. And he is to observe and follow such orders and directions as he shall receive from his military superiors, according to the rules and discipline of War.

Given under my hand at Maxwell Field, Alabama this Fifteenth day of January in the year of Our Lord one thousand nine hundred and Forty-three.

MARK C. BANE, JR.,
Captain, Air Corps,

Commandant of Aviation Cadets

Aviation Cadet Form No. 31 SEAAFTC

While at Maxwell Field I was appointed Cadet Corporal which was probably due to my two years of ROTC at VPI.

One thing I didn't care for was being confined to the barracks area and not allowed to go anywhere unless I marched with a cadet officer. We marched to all meals, to all classes, to exercise, and even to the movies.

I was doing well with my classes, and my grades permitted me to go to the movies any evening I wished. The shows cost fifteen cents and several of us would go every night. The guys who were not getting good grades had to stay in the barracks and study.

Aviation cadet pay was $75.00 a month. Deductions were taken which I did not always understand. I sent money home to pay on my debt to Tech. I usually had about $35.00 left for my own use. It does not seem like much now, but at the time I had more spending money left than ever before.

The army had a unique and antique system for paying troops. Each squadron lined up alphabetically, and each man approached a table where the pay officer was seated with a couple of armed MPs standing behind him. The table was covered with a brown wool GI blanket and a .45 automatic pistol as a center piece. When the soldier to be paid signed a payment book, the officer handed him cash. I never received a pay check in the three years

I was in service; I was always paid in cash. I have been told this pay procedure was still in use even during the Korean War.

We were kept very busy during the week, but received a 24-hour leave each weekend. Saturday morning we exercised, had room inspection, and from noon until noon Sunday, we were on our own. There was not much to do except ride a bus into Montgomery, and walk around the downtown area, which my roommates and I did every Saturday afternoon. We looked forward to a restaurant meal. It was here that I discovered "sizzling steak." This $1.65 menu item was served on a heated iron platter and I thought I had found "Shangri-La." We always returned to the base in time for supper.

Sunday we usually slept until noon, and a parade was always scheduled for the afternoon. I suppose it was nice to watch but extremely boring for those of us who marched, and torture to those who happened to have partied too much on Saturday night.

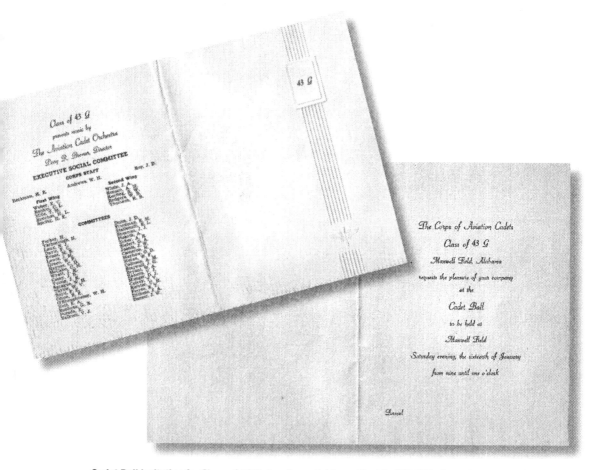

Cadet Ball invitation for Class of 43 G showing outside and inside. "43 G" indicated the year 1943 and that they were the "G" group of cadets amongst the many groups who rotated through Maxwell Field, Alabama during training.

Somewhere here I met a private and we began to talk about our pay. We each knew what the other received. This soldier had been in the service several years without a promotion. He said "When I get paid, I divide it into three parts. I spend one-third on liquor, one-third on women, and the third part I spend foolishly." This was my picture of a peace-time soldier.

The highlight of my stay at Maxwell Field was being able to attend a concert played by Captain Glenn Miller and his newly formed Army Air Corps Band.

Almost before I knew it, our twelve-week stay at Maxwell Field came to a close. At the graduation ceremony, it was announced that our squadron would be going to primary flying school in Decatur, Alabama.

A formal Cadet Ball with a live band was planned for Saturday evening. For some reason that I cannot recall, neither I nor any of my roommates chose to attend the ball.

Two days later I again boarded a train, bound for my next great adventure.

The table was covered with a brown wool GI blanket and a .45 automatic pistol as a center piece. When the soldier to be paid signed a payment book, the officer handed him cash.
I never received a pay check in the three years I was in service; I was always paid in cash.

CHAPTER 4

Primary Pilot School

Decatur, Alabama

1943 February

Decatur was a nice, small, southern town on Wheeler Lake, which had been formed by damming the Tennessee River, and it looked very pretty from the air.

Again, I was pleasantly surprised by our living quarters. The buildings were brick and there were only four men to each room. We were assigned quarters alphabetically, both here and at Maxwell Field so I was well acquainted with my roommates and those on either side of my room.

The meals were excellent, a tremendous improvement over the last station. I expected I would gain some weight while here. The flying school was privately owned and leased by the Army Air Corps. It operated with civilian instructors and I began to feel quite comfortable on this base and looked forward to the training program.

No time was wasted beginning training. Right off the bat on Monday morning, we were issued flying clothes, an A-2 jacket (which I still have) and all the heavy sheepskin garments including boots, mittens, and helmet. We were scheduled to be in ground school half a day, and on the flight line the other half. Therefore I would be indoors

1943. Looking for the wild blue yonder.

in the morning and in the air after lunch and all afternoon.

Ground school was similar to Maxwell Field, except far more intensive. The emphasis was on an airplane's component systems, mainly the electrical, hydraulic, and flight controls. As at Maxwell, the ground school caused me no problem.

My first time on the flight line was an overwhelming experience. Five cadets were assigned to each instructor, and all of our last names starting with O or P. Our instructor was Sam McGuffin, a civilian from Waynesboro, Virginia, and I liked him immediately.

We began by learning the flight line rules and procedures. There must have been a thousand dos and don'ts to remember. We were introduced to the airplane, a Stearman, known as a PT-17 to the Air Corps. It was an open cockpit, two-seat bi-plane, with a 220-horsepower radial engine. I was overly awed by this monster. We took turns sitting in the back seat having the instruments and controls explained to us. The instruments were easy, since there were only three: an altimeter, a compass, and a tachometer. The gasoline was in the top wing with a glass fuel indicator hanging down from it. The controls looked easy. Pull back on the stick to go up, and push forward to go down, all the time using the right foot on the right rudder pedal to go right, or the left pedal to go left. Now I realized why we had been given so many coordination tests back in Nashville.

To start the engine the cadet took a crank out of the rear cockpit, inserted it onto the starter, an opening in the side of the engine, and began cranking. This was not easy, for one cranked until it wound up, then jumped clear while the pilot in the front seat engaged the engine. One scrambled into the back seat with the crank in hand hoping the engine would fire, or else he would have to repeat the cranking. After fastening the seat belt, he secured the crank in its holder. If it were not put in correctly, it would come whizzing by the cadet's head, any time he was upside down doing acrobatic maneuvers.

The first day closed with a visit to the parachute shop. We tried on "chutes" and learned how they functioned and how to operate them. We were told, "It don't mean a thing,

1943. I was issued this jacket at Decatur. It's not very shiny now, but I still have it and I can still get into it!!

if you don't pull that string." The chutes were all seat packs, which meant they hung below your butt and banged the back of your knees as you walked. It was very uncomfortable to sit on since it fit into the seat, and it became a hard cushion during the flight. These seats were the original "bucket seats."

Of the five students assigned to Sam McGuffin, one had been a crop duster, and he appeared to be an experienced pilot. None of the other four had ever flown before and the first time one of the others went up he was scared so badly, he started banging the side of the cockpit yelling, "Let me out of here." That was his last day as a cadet.

Several days later another student taxied into a large plywood sign and broke the propeller, throwing wood splinters over a large area. That was his last day as a cadet. I do not know what happened to the third cadet, but within a week Sam was down to two students, the crop duster who needed no help, and myself who needed lots of help.

02 February, 1943 was the date of my first-ever airplane ride, and simultaneously my first flying lesson. Sam sat in the front seat and I rode in the rear seat. An antique instrument called a Gosport Tube was our high-tech mode of communication. It consisted of a small funnel inserted into a length of rubber tubing, which went from the front seat to the rear seat and branched into two smaller tubes, which went into the ear holes in my helmet. Sam would yell into the funnel, and I was supposed hear what he was saying. No intelligible word ever came through that contraption. With that 220 horsepower up front and the wind whistling by at 60 mph, communication was limited. I had no way of talking back to him, so the system was a one-way street. The bulky mittens I wore prevented any hand signals but he had a small rear view mirror, so he could see if I was throwing up, had fallen out, or was experiencing any other difficulty.

From the first minute in the plane until we landed I was being taught something. We were always up there doing something. Before we took off, Sam would describe what we would be doing that afternoon. Once we were in flight, he would describe what he was doing, or what he was going to do. He instructed that he would do it once, and then I would repeat it. He would look into the mirror for my reaction, but with that big fur collar covering my chin and mouth, and goggles covering my eyes, all he could see was my nose and there was not much information visible. As he was doing the maneuver, I would put my hands and feet lightly on the controls in front of me to follow along. When he had done it once, he would put his elbows over the edge of the cockpit to demonstrate the controls were all mine.

I suppose military flying instruction was much different than civilian lessons. We never flew straight and level, but were always involved in some sort of maneuver. My first lesson was to find a straight road with a crosswind. I was to fly back and forth across it, making equidistant loops on either side of it. I was to compensate for the wind by making tighter turns on the downwind side, and loose ones on the upwind leg. The next lesson was to find a crossroad, and do figure-eights over it, and again compensating for the wind.

Alabama in February was not the "Sunny South." An open cockpit was cold, or I could say, downright frigid. I do not think I knew what a wind-chill factor was, but I knew it was low. Our flying clothes were very bulky, and I believe we could have been warmer in some sort of layered outfit. Sam had a chamois skin facemask that looked pretty cozy. I was usually shivering and tense, and when Sam noticed, he would motion me to get off the controls, and he would do a couple of snap rolls, or slow rolls, or fly upside down. That experience always warmed me up.

During the second week of instruction, Sam told me he would show me how to stall the plane, put it into a spin, and recover control. All our flying had been at 500 feet, but now we would go up to 3,000 feet for this exercise. We flew to altitude, and found a long straight road to perform on. He lined up on the road and slowly pulled back on the stick, while slowly cutting the throttle. Just as the nose was pointing straight up, the engine died, the controls went limp and he kicked the rudder. We fell off on one wing, and started spinning. After a turn and a half he kicked the opposite rudder to stop the spin, pushed the stick forword, gave the engine some gas, and as we gained air speed, he pulled back on the stick. We found ourselves flying straight and level down that same road. I was enjoying all this until he said, "Take it back up and you do one." I took my good old time climbing back up as I was trying to remember every thing he had told me. We got up along that same road and he motioned for me to begin. Well, without any thought, I jerked the stick and cut the throttle. That Stearman shot straight up in the air and as it stalled, I kicked the rudder. The plane fell over on its back, and started spinning. I had inadvertently inverted us. I glanced up to see how Sam was going to get us out of this mess, but he was just sitting there with his elbows on the edge of the cockpit, enjoying the scenery spinning past us. I finally kicked the rudder to stop the spin, and worked the stick and throttle to get us back straight and level. He motioned for me to go back up and try again. I did several more that afternoon, but none as spectacular as the first.

Well, without any thought, I jerked the stick and cut the throttle. That Stearman shot straight up in the air and as it stalled, I kicked the rudder. The plane fell over on its back, and started spinning. I had inadvertently inverted us.

Stearman PT-17, primary trainer. Many thousand aviation cadets started out on this plane.

Once I seemed to have the stall problem under control, we began to work on take-off and landing. This was done at an auxiliary landing strip, several miles away from the main base. I guess they did not want any crashes where there would be witnesses. The wheels on a Stearman were close together, and with a full fuel load in the top wing, the plane was top heavy and likely to tip over. A pilot had to be very quick on the rudder pedals, while taxiing, taking off, or landing. If one was not careful, you could find yourself in a ground loop, which meant the plane was pivoting on one wheel, with the end of the wing dragging the ground and dissolving into sticks, strings, and fabric. One day I performed this ground loop maneuver on the main base. The result meant I had to go to the hospital for an eye examination before I would be cleared to return to flying instruction.

I began to realize that I was not becoming the world's greatest pilot, and previously Sam had informed me I was no "hot rock."

02 March we were at the auxiliary field shooting landings. I had three or four rounds and when I taxied back to the take-off point, Sam told me to wait a minute. He calmly unbuckled his seat belt and parachute, and stepped out of the plane and told me to take it around by myself. I had not expected to solo so soon but I took a deep breath, and took off. I landed and he told me to do it three more times, after which we returned to the main base. I guess this was the happiest day of my life. I had soloed an airplane. I had never been in an airplane

---

If one was not careful, you could find yourself in a ground loop, which meant the plane was pivoting on one wheel, with the end of the wing dragging the ground and dissolving into sticks, strings, and fabric.

---

until 30 days before, and I had never had a driver's license. After nine hours of flying time, I had done it. I never even knew of any one who had soloed an airplane before they learned to drive an automobile.

That evening I talked with Sam about the day. He said, "We had at stake, your life, my reputation, and a $17,000 airplane. I was going to be darn sure you knew what you were doing, before I let you go up alone."

The next day we returned to the auxiliary field, where I made many more take-offs and landings. The following day he had me do a few more, and told me to take it up to 3,000 feet and do some solo stalls and spins. This took all the courage I could muster, but I bit the bullet and did it, and amazed myself by doing it well.

We continued to practice everything I had been taught, including many new things. One thing though, was a nuisance. As we would be flying along, he would yell "crash landing." I was constantly supposed to be looking for a place to land in case the engine quit, but of course, I was concentrating on whatever else I was doing, and never had a location picked out for a dead-stick landing.

Things were going along pretty well, although I had quit thinking of myself in the same class as Jimmy Doolittle or Charles Lindbergh. Disaster struck suddenly when I ground looped twice in one day. That meant two embarrassing trips to the hospital for eye examinations. I knew the Air Corps took a very dim view of pilots who tore the wings off of two airplanes in one day.

On March 22nd I was scheduled for a check ride with one of the Army pilots stationed there. The one checking me was a captain, and he ran me through everything I had been taught. Nothing went very well on that ride, and when he told me to go to the base, I was lost and couldn't find Decatur Field. We finally landed and as we walked back to the ready room, he put his arm around me and said, "Son, I certainly hope you can get into something for which you are better suited." That captain was a real gentleman in the way he terminated my career as a pilot. I was mad, disappointed, embarrassed, devastated, and everything else. That was the first time in my life that I failed something I really wanted.

A day or two later I found myself with several "washed out" cadets at the train station waiting to be returned to Nashville. I met with a classification officer there who told me

---

I guess this was the happiest day of my life. I had soloed an airplane. I had never been in an airplane until 30 days before, and I had never had a driver's license.

A Stearman PT-17 shown in flight. I always rode in the rear seat, even when I soloed.

that in addition to qualifying for pilot training, I had also qualified for bombardier and navigation training, and did I have a preference. I told him I would like to go to navigation school. A couple of days later, a Sunday, around five o'clock in the afternoon, I was taking a shower when another cadet burst in and said the squadron commander wanted to see me immediately, and that didn't mean five minutes from now. The captain told me a train was leaving in one hour, and I better be on it when it left. I was soaking wet, I had clothes in the laundry which I couldn't get and I was flat broke because I had missed a payday in moving here from Decatur. Fortunately, another cadet who I had only known for a few days loaned me ten dollars. I was to wear my coveralls and pack everything else except toilet articles in my barracks bags.

The train was long, and there must have been hundreds of us on it. Our bags were all in the baggage cars which we couldn't access. The train left on time, destination unknown. We drew numbers for berths, and I was lucky enough to draw an upper berth. The unlucky ones had to sleep two to a lower berth. Rumors abounded as to where we were going, but all I could tell was we were headed west, sometimes northwest, and sometimes southwest, but always west. About the third day the train stopped in a very desolate place (I think we were in Nebraska), and we were ordered off the train. Believe it or not, we were surrounded by armed MPs while we were required to do about a half hour of calisthenics. The MPs were totally unnecessary as I do not think anyone had an idea of escaping into that wilderness. Later that day rumor said we were near Cheyenne, Wyoming, and then it started to snow and soon we were in a real blizzard. It got very cold on the train and as we had only coveralls to wear, we began to get mighty chilly. They finally let us put down the sleeping berths. The next day we passed though Salt Lake City and headed SW again. All this changing of direction did nothing to squelch the rumors and conjecture as to our final destination. The next day found us traveling though Nevada in the most bleak scenery I had ever viewed. That afternoon we passed a group of army tanks having shooting practice. We could see them firing cannons and the shells bursting on the side of a distant mountain. The next morning, a Saturday, we awoke to more desert but shortly the scenery turned green, and at noon the train pulled into an Army base. I was mighty happy to get off the train, as we had run out of food and our last two meals had been cornflakes with milk.

On the train ride from Nashville I became reconciled to the fact that I would not be getting pilot wings. I consoled myself by thinking I should not have expected to since I had never been in an airplane before and never driven an automobile. I was determined that I would work hard to get my navigator wings. Later on I learned that two-thirds of my pilot class at Decatur had washed out, so I was not the only disappointed one.

A couple of days later, a Sunday, around five o'clock in the afternoon, I was taking a shower when another cadet burst in and said the squadron commander wanted to see me immediately, and that didn't mean five minutes from now. The captain told me a train was leaving in one hour, and I better be on it when it left.

CHAPTER 5

Pre-Flight School... Again

Santa Ana, California

1943 April

Getting off the train at noon in California, we were welcomed to the Santa Ana Army Air Base. As at Nashville the previous October, our first stop was the mess hall. I cannot remember what we ate, but I know I surely enjoyed it.

One of the first things I learned was that this was another pre-flight school and after twelve weeks here, I would be going on to bombardier school. BOMBARDIER SCHOOL! What ever happened to navigation school? I should have known the army never gives you what you ask for. Well, I was stuck here and I might as well make the best of it.

It did not take me long to fall in love with this base. The climate was wonderful, the base was attractive, the food was first class. There were crates of fresh navel oranges along the food-service line, and the most amazing thing of all, at the end of the line was a dip-it-your-

> *One of the first things I learned was that this was another pre-flight school and after twelve weeks here, I would be going on to bombardier school. BOMBARDIER SCHOOL! What ever happened to navigation school?*

self freezer of ice cream. A huge bowl of frozen strawberries to ladle over the ice cream was placed next to the freezer. I had never seen frozen strawberries before and I thought this might be heaven on earth.

I fell into the routine quite easily. It was pretty much a repeat of what I had experienced

A classmate and Art in a penny arcade while visiting Balboa Beach at Santa Ana, California

before at Maxwell Field, with less emphasis on engines and aerodynamics. More on navigation, meteorology, aircraft identification, and weapons, especially machine guns.

I have vague memories of Morse code class. We had to learn all the "dits" and "dashes" of this code. To send and receive a "word" consisting of five letters, we started by shooting for five words a minute. It took me quite a while to achieve this; then my goal became eight words a minute. The eight words came easily. I was told in order to pass I now had to send ten words per minute. I really struggled. Code class was the only part of ground school that gave me any trouble.

During the first or second week I was in Santa Ana, they exchanged the enlisted man/cadet type blouse for one very similar to an officer's. This was a nice improvement. I had a difficult time getting replacement uniform parts to replace the laundry I had to leave in Nashville and I think I wore my one outfit for two weeks before I got a new set. I was the only man wearing wool pants in the California heat and I really stood out when we were in formation.

To my surprise one day, I recognized the guy who had loaned me the $10.00 back in Nashville. He said he was sent out here two weeks after I was. I repaid him and told him I was sorry he had to come across the continent to get his money back.

Calisthenics were with us again but there was practically no running. We were still restricted to the barracks area, and marched in groups everywhere we went. The base rules stated that we had to sing whenever we marched, and I got terribly tired of "Off We Go Into The Wild Blue Yonder" and "I've Got Sixpence, Jolly, Jolly Sixpence," these being the only songs everyone knew.

Like Maxwell Field, we were allowed a 24-hour leave every weekend. The favorite destinations were the towns of Laguna and Balboa Beaches on the Pacific Ocean. To thwart a Japanese landing in California, the beaches were off limits and covered with barbed wire. Both places were overwhelmed by men in uniform and it really was not much fun.

One afternoon four of us rented a small sailboat for an hour of cruising on the bay. The wind was blowing in from the ocean, and none of us had any idea how to sail the boat back to the dock when our hour was up. The owner was noticeably mad when he had come out in a motor boat to tow us back to the dock.

Like Maxwell Field, we had a parade every Sunday afternoon. Usually a large number of cadets had spent the night at the beach and returned with hangovers. Standing at attention in that scorching California sun was pure torture for the revelers and they dropped like flyboys.

One day an announcement stated that the squadron which won the Sunday Parade would be honored the following Saturday night at The Hollywood Party of the Masquers Club. We received first place in the parade and on Saturday we were bussed to Los Angeles.

We obtained lodging in an American Legion Hall and headed for the party. Our waiters were members of the club, and although none of them were big stars, I had seen most of them in the movies. The star of the show was comedian Jack Benny supported by the entire cast of the Jack Benny Radio Show, Claudette Colbert, Danny Kaye, Hedda Hopper, Joe E. Brown, and others. All these stars have now moved on to the big stage in the heavens.

After dinner, the entertainers went to the head table. We filed in front of the stars and obtained their autographs on our souvenir dinner menu. I still treasure that menu and the memory of that evening.

Back at Santa Ana, classes continued. They repeated most of what I had learned at Maxwell Field including the gas mask drill, the high altitude chamber, and the firing range. The Santa Ana range was located on the beach and we fired out into the Pacific Ocean. I often wondered how many fish died of lead poisoning.

Twelve weeks at Santa Ana were coming to a close and all too soon. I really liked this place. I breezed through the classes, went to the movies almost every night, enjoyed the good food, gained weight, and got a good suntan. The town of Santa Ana with its palm trees, orange groves, and gorgeous weather was quite removed from Covington, Virginia, with its aromatic paper mill and gloomy weather.

At the end of June a few more than a hundred of us were transported by busses across the San Bernardino Mountains to Victorville, California, Army Air Base to commence Bombardier School.

A FRONT ROW SEAT AT THE WAR

CHAPTER 6

Bombardier School

Victorville, California

1943 July

Victorville was located in the middle of the Mojave Desert not far from Death Valley. The air base was OK but after viewing the surrounding country, I concluded the only thing it was good for was to drop bombs on.

The accommodations were good, consisting of two-story barracks cut into real rooms with four cadets per room. The latrines were on the first floor. The food was excellent and without a doubt the best I had at any base during my entire military experience.

My recollection was arrival on a Saturday, getting settled on Sunday, and on Monday morning, right to work. The ground school was a continuation of the subjects studied at Santa Ana, but with additional classes on bombing theory, aircraft and naval vessel identification, Morse code, and the Norden bombsight.

The famous and highly secret Norden bombsight was a marvel to me. I was totally in awe. Norden developed his brainchild during the 1920s and '30s for the Navy. The Navy found no use for it and relied chiefly on dive bombing. Consequently the army adopted the device, and in the 1930s the Boeing Company designed the B-17 airplane around it for use

Norden developed his brainchild during the 1920s and '30s for the Navy. The Navy found no use for it and relied chiefly on dive bombing. Consequently the army adopted the device, and in the 1930s the Boeing Company designed the B-17 airplane around it for use in high altitude level bombing.

in high altitude level bombing.

Norden's design used an optimal bombing altitude of 11,000 feet estimating that it would be above any enemy anti-aircraft fire. If it was used much below 11,000 feet, the ground would move too fast under the telescope and above that altitude the margin of error would increase correspondingly.

In Europe the normal bombing altitude for the Eighth Air Force was 24,000 feet and accuracy suffered, and we were never above the range of the German guns.

The Norden bombsight was shaped like a loaf of sandwich bread, but larger. It was portable and when in use was positioned on top of the auto pilot, sometimes called "George." It was a sophisticated, mechanical calculator full of electrical wiring including a gyroscope, a telescope, two small motors, and miscellaneous "stuff." The bombardier fed a number of items of information into it, duplicating the ground speed, and at the crucial instant, it sent a signal to the bomb bay and the bombs were released. This marvelous piece of equipment filled me with determination to master it.

We had a course in Norden bombsight maintenance and repair but at the end were told keep our fingers out of it and let the experts attend to any problems. These experts were all privates first class (PFC) and I thought any one who could repair one of those instruments should be a master sergeant or at least a Lieutenant Colonel.

The Norden bombsight was shaped like a loaf of sandwich bread, but larger. It was portable and when in use was positioned on top of the auto pilot, sometimes called "George." It was a sophisticated, mechanical calculator full of electrical wiring including a gyroscope, a telescope, two small motors, and miscellaneous "stuff."

Within a few days, we started instruction in the bomb trainers, which were located in a large hangar and looked like metal scaffolds on wheels. About twelve feet up was a platform which held the bombsight, auto pilot, and seats for the instructor and the cadet. My instructor was a 2nd Lt. Boone who claimed to be a direct descendent of Daniel Boone. He attempted to be rough and tough, but actually he was a very nice guy.

The first thing I noticed about the Norden was a thick black foam rubber ring around the eyepiece. The bombardier's head actually rested on it while working. In an airplane sitting out on the concrete, in a temperature over a hundred degrees, the foam would get soft and sticky and leave a big black ring around the eye of the user.

Lt. Boone showed and explained all the dials, switches, knobs, bells, whistles, and smoke

NOMENCLATURE AND OPERATION

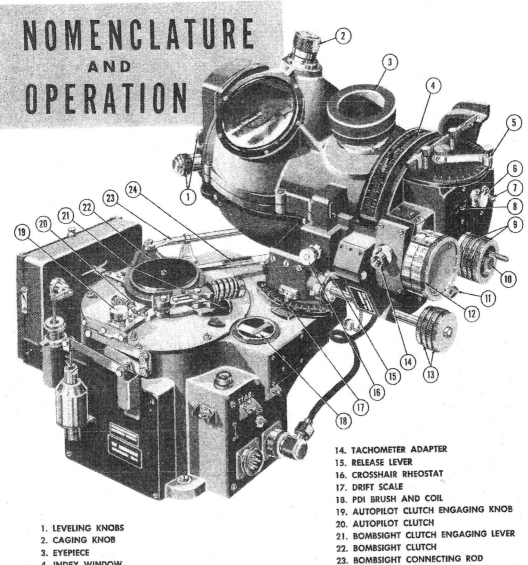

1. LEVELING KNOBS
2. CAGING KNOB
3. EYEPIECE
4. INDEX WINDOW
5. TRAIL ARM AND TRAIL PLATE
6. EXTENDED VISION KNOB
7. RATE MOTOR SWITCH
8. DISC SPEED GEAR SHIFT
9. RATE AND DISPLACEMENT KNOBS
10. MIRROR DRIVE CLUTCH
11. SEARCH KNOB
12. DISC SPEED DRUM
13. TURN AND DRIFT KNOBS
14. TACHOMETER ADAPTER
15. RELEASE LEVER
16. CROSSHAIR RHEOSTAT
17. DRIFT SCALE
18. PDI BRUSH AND COIL
19. AUTOPILOT CLUTCH ENGAGING KNOB
20. AUTOPILOT CLUTCH
21. BOMBSIGHT CLUTCH ENGAGING LEVER
22. BOMBSIGHT CLUTCH
23. BOMBSIGHT CONNECTING ROD
24. AUTOPILOT CONNECTING ROD

The bombsight has 2 main parts, **sighthead** and **stabilizer**. The sighthead pivots on the stabilizer and is locked to it by the dovetail locking pin. The sighthead is connected to the directional gyro in the stabilizer through the **bombsight connecting rod** and the **bombsight clutch**.

RESTRICTED   MARCH, 1946 BIF 5-1-1

NOMENCLATURE AND FUNCTIONING

STABILIZER

1. DIRECTIONAL ARM LOCK
2. DASHPOT
3. DIRECTIONAL PANEL
4. DIRECTIONAL PANEL ARM
5. AUTOPILOT CLUTCH ARM EXTENSION
6. AUTOPILOT CLUTCH
7. AUTOPILOT CONNECTING ROD
8. DRIFT GEAR CLUTCH
9. PDI
10. BOMBSIGHT CLUTCH

DIRECTIONAL PANEL

1. RUDDER PICKUP POT AND WIPER
2. SLIDING BLOCK
3. ERECTING CUTOUT SWITCH
4. DUAL BANKING POT AND WIPERS

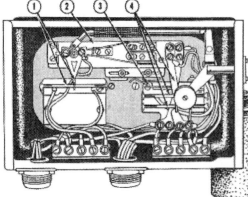

Stabilizer

The directional gyro of the bombsight stabilizer detects any deviation of an airplane from **straight** flight. The autopilot clutch connects the directional gyro to the directional panel. The directional panel, attached to the side of the bombsight stabilizer, measures electrically the deviations which the directional gyro notes. Signals then are produced which direct the servo units to correct the deviation.

If you want to steer the airplane by the autopilot clutch, disengage it. This disconnects the directional gyro from the directional panel. Now, you are in control of the directional panel and, through it, you also control the servo units. When you move the autopilot clutch you cause the airplane to turn.

The airplane resumes straight and level flight when you again engage the autopilot clutch to the directional gyro, or when you return the clutch to center by hand.

The directional arm lock prevents the directional panel from cancelling out signals put in by the turn control when you are using it to make a turn. When the turn control is moved from CENTER, the solenoid of the directional arm lock causes the clamping jaws to lock the autopilot clutch arm in position. The autopilot clutch slips throughout the turn. As soon as you put the turn control back in CENTER, the autopilot clutch enables the directional gyro to stabilize the airplane on its new heading.

The dashpot is linked to the mechanism in the directional panel which produces the signal for rudder control. It increases the signal for initial rudder correction as the speed of the airplane's yaw increases. You can govern the extent of increase in that signal by adjusting the knurled nut on top of the dashpot.

RESTRICTED

and mirrors. As he was doing this, I decided it would take a minimum of three hands, and ideally five or six, to work this instrument. As one looked through the eye piece, you were looking down through a telescope attached to a gyroscope. This gyro rotated at a very high rate of speed and its function was to keep the telescope in a perfectly vertical position. The airplane and the rest of the bombsight could roll, be nose up, nose down, turn, or whatever, but the telescope remained at that vertical position. The problem was when should the bombs be dropped. If the plane was flying at 240 mph, it was moving 4 miles per minute, and if the bombs were dropped 15 seconds early or late, the target would be missed by a mile. Timing

The only "tree" on the base

was everything, and the Norden bombsight dropped the bombs at the correct time.

In looking through the telescope one sees a cross-hair, and with a tilting mirror straight ahead toward the target. The bombardier's task is to keep the cross-hairs on the target, by manipulating four knobs, two in each hand. The bombsight does the rest. Gyroscopes are endowed with the property of "rigidity in space" and if one watches for a while, you notice it beginning to tilt. The gyroscope however, maintains its position in space and the rotation of the earth makes it seem to move. The same thing happens to the gyro in the bombsight. The plane and the earth below might move but the gyro and telescope stayed fixed. There are

---

The problem was when should the bombs be dropped. If the plane was flying at 240 mph, it was moving 4 miles per minute, and if the bombs were dropped 15 seconds early or late, the target would be missed by a mile.

---

two liquid-filled levels attached to the gyro, one fore and aft, and one crossways. Two "precession" knobs were attached to the gyroscope, and when the bubble in the levels showed it was off level, one trued it up using gyroscope bubbles and the cross-hair knobs. The bombardier did not need to think about actually dropping the bomb because the bombsight did it automatically at the right time. Usually I was still making corrections when the bomb dropped. If everything was right the bomb would hit the target. If the plane was flying too high or accelerating, the bomb would overshoot and if it was low or decelerating, it would fall short. Generally the gremlins were in the bubbles. One needed a sixth sense about them and had to decide if they were lying.

The gyroscope could be perfectly level but if the plane was accelerating, the bubble would be at the front. In trying to get back to the center of the tube you would unbalance it which threw your crosshair off the target and in putting it back on you gave it a wrong signal, and you would miss the target. Having been told all this and a lot more, I tried it out on the bomb trainer. This contraption on wheels moved slowly across the floor, and I aimed at a box about a foot in size on the floor. There was a paper bull's eye target on the box. As it rolled over an electric solenoid plunger stabbed down to mark where a bomb would have hit. The rest of the day was spent practicing this simulated bomb run.

Two or three days later the box on the floor also was set in motion to simulate a moving target or cross winds. By the end of the first week of training Lt. Boone said I was ready to try it from a real airplane. At 11,000 feet altitude. At Decatur we never flew higher than 3,000 feet.

Somewhere along the way it dawned on me that nothing about the Norden bombsight was documented. No training manuals, no handouts, no diagrams, or pictures. Every thing was taught orally and the student had to memorize it. All for the sake of highest security.

The flying bomb trainer designated an AT-17 was a twin engine Beechcraft that carried a crew of four: a pilot, the bombing instructor, two cadets, and ten 100-pound bombs. We received an extensive briefing from the instructor and the pilot and then checked out all of our gear including a parachute, maps, ballistic charts, circular slide-rule, calculators, a tachometer, and a 16-mm movie camera. We wore coveralls and (unlined) A-2 jackets. We trooped out to the plane and the first duty was to pre-flight the bombsight. This took about fifteen minutes. The plane was sitting there in that Mojave Desert sunshine on a concrete ramp and the temperature inside that metal cocoon often reached 130 degrees. The pilot was screaming for me to finish, the instructor was trying to teach me something, and I was ready to pass out.

Take-off was a welcome relief, and when we reached 11,000 feet, the bombing altitude, the temperature had dropped to 30 degrees. That 100-degree drop did nothing to make anyone in the plane happier because it was now freezing.

Each cadet would fly a course of five targets and drop a bomb on each, and would then trade places with the other cadet, who would drop the remaining five bombs. Each bomb contained 95 pounds of sand and five pounds of black powder in the tail. When the bomb hit, the black powder would detonate, forming a big puff of smoke, which was easily seen from the plane. This target was a 20' x 20' square which we called the "shack." I visualized a wooden building but later found out it was a pile of whitewashed rocks. Outward from the shack were five concentric white circles, one at 50 feet and the others at 100, 200, 300, and 500 feet.

While one cadet was dropping his bombs, the other one was inserting the camera in a hole in the floor at the rear of the plane, taking pictures of the bomb hits (or misses). To win wings, we had to have a circular error (CE) of less than 230 feet and we could always arrange with our buddy to "accidentally" miss pictures of any wild bombs or ones that would fall outside of the circles.

The back of the training plane was an uncomfortable place. It was always in motion, swinging from side to side to side, bouncing up and down, or making circles. This movement produced quite a bit of distress for the cameraman. Air sickness was common and one of the first things we learned was not to throw up through the camera hole, because a regular gale was blowing into the plane. A knowing man would use his cap and gently ease it out of the hole. The desert floor was probably littered with those caps.

Several of my classmates washed out due to airsickness but fortunately, it never bothered me. I believe I had an advantage over many of them, in that flying was no novelty. Those of us who had experienced pilot training were not afraid of the plane. Many of the cadets had never flown before, and trying to use a bombsight on the first time aloft must have been a gut-wrenching experience.

The bombsight was transported by hand in a canvas satchel. I do not know what it weighed, but I think 25 to 30 pounds. It was carried out to the plane, set in place, and the gyro turned on to start the pre-flight inspection. Upon landing it was returned in the bag to the vault. The motor had been cut off but the gyro was still rotating at a high rate of speed and if one had to turn a corner, it vigorously resisted the turn. One had to grab that bag and with all one's strength twist it 90 degrees or else it would stick out from the body and be very awkward to carry.

The village of Victorville was any thing but a tourist Mecca, and other than a bar called "The Green Spot" and a couple of small stores, the only place to go on a Saturday night was the local school. The United Service Organization (USO) had set up some diversions including ping-pong tables, a pool table, etc. for us. One night I was playing ping-pong, when everything started shaking, and rumbling. I stood there like a dummy while everyone else made a mad dash for the exits. Having never been in an earthquake, I did not know what was happening. In a minute or so, after no noticeable damage, everyone came back inside and we resumed our games.

I had recently purchased sunglasses to make myself look like a hot pilot. I had them in my hip pocket. I lunged to hit a ball, slipped, sat on my new glasses, smashing them, and they had cost $12. That was the last time I went to the USO.

During World War II, Bob Hope went to every outpost in the Pacific but he never got to Victorville, and it was only a half-hour plane ride.

One thing I liked about this base was the absence of calisthenics. We ran some but not as much as we did at Maxwell Field. During our exercise periods, we could play volleyball, basketball, pitch horseshoes, or do some other things. The most attractive choice for me was a row of punching bags, mounted on posts.

During the second month of our training we switched from daytime bombing to nighttime. By now, we were familiar enough with the bombsight to operate it without looking

...I was called into the orderly room where a captain told me my parents had received a telegram from the Navy, informing them that my brother Bob had been reported missing in action. This was devastating news and totally unexpected. He went on to say the Red Cross had requested a two-week leave of absence for me and they would provide a round trip train ticket for me to go home.

at our hands. I did it automatically, without thinking, and to make it easier, the target and surrounding circles were all lit up.

After we had completed a night flight and were released to go back to the barracks, we detoured to the mess hall, where an automatic doughnut machine was spewing out "sinkers" and an urn of hot Ovaltine awaited. I would eat several doughnuts, down a couple of cups of Ovaltine, go to bed, and sleep like a baby. It would get cold in the desert at night, but I never had any trouble sleeping.

A detachment of Women's Army Air Corps (WAACs) did all the paper work connected with our bombing. They developed the film we had shot and measured where our bombs hit and calculated our CEs. They were real nice elderly ladies and I'll bet some of them were as much as 40 years old!

About nine weeks into my training here, I was called into the orderly room where a captain told me my parents had received a telegram from the Navy, informing them that my brother Bob had been reported missing in action. This was devastating news and totally unexpected. He went on to say the Red Cross had requested a two-week leave of absence for me and they would provide a round trip train ticket for me to go home.

Bob was barely twenty years old. He had enlisted in the Navy a few weeks after Pearl Harbor and was sent to boot camp in Norfolk, Virginia. After additional training, he was rated a Torpedoman third class. He had been stationed aboard the cruiser, *San Juan*, and had been involved in several naval engagements. When the *San Juan* was severely damaged in the Pacific, Bob was transferred to the destroyer *Maddox*. He saw service in the North Atlantic and off the west coast of Africa. When the Allies defeated the Germans in North Africa and were crossing the Mediterranean, the *Maddox* was there to assist in the landings at Sicily. According to the survivors, the *Maddox* took a hit from a German bomb and sank immediately.

A year later, the Navy sent my parents a Purple Heart and a telegram saying Bob was presumed dead. While visiting the US Military Cemetery in Cambridge, England, in 1984, I learned from their records that Bob's name and date of death, 1944 July is inscribed on The Wall of the Dead in the US Cemetery, Palermo, Italy.

It was a sad and miserable train ride from Victorville back to Virginia. The railroad cars must have been borrowed from a museum. There was no cooling to ease that hot August sun. The windows were wide open and black smoke from the engines covered everything. There were more passengers than seats and if you had a seat, you held it until you were desperate to get to the toilet. When you returned, someone else was in your seat.

There was no dining car and several times a day the train would stop at some small town where everyone rushed into the train station to find something to eat. It took three days to get to Chicago, where I changed to a more modern train. I think I slept all the way from there to Covington, Virginia, where I arrived the next day.

I had not been home since I entered the service, ten months before, and it was a sad reunion with my parents, two brothers, and sister. I spent much of my time at home and catching up on my sleep. I tried to find some high school friends but most of them were gone, involved in the war effort. Before I knew it, my leave was over and I had to return to Victorville.

After another long train ride, I was back at Victorville. My class was graduating at the end of the week so I was put back into class 43-14. This meant a different squadron, new barracks, new roommates, and a new instructor.

In my absence I had been awarded a Good Conduct Medal, and now I had a red ribbon to wear on my otherwise drab uniform. As a rule, the cadets were a very well behaved bunch of guys. We realized we had better watch our steps because the Army would not put up with any foolishness. We had a lot to lose. We all wanted those wings and commissions, and nobody wanted to "wash out" due to bad behavior. Even today, I believe those cadets were the greatest group of young men I have ever known.

My new instructor and I got along fine. I was comfortable with the bombsight and felt I had conquered it. It was fun and I imagined it as a game, something like today's computer games. All I had to do was keep those cross-hairs on the target and "bingo."

A week later, we moved out into the desert for war maneuvers. We slept in eight-man squad tents, ate out of mess kits, and forgot about bathing. The accommodations were primitive. We continued our bomb runs and other classroom activities. A couple of our instructors were veterans of the recent fighting in North Africa and I think they were preparing us for the "year before the war." A firing range was set up and we had to make practice shots for a shooting badge with the .45 automatic pistol. We had to come to the range every day until we were qualified. I do not think the sergeants were too eager to be out there every day and I think they sometimes "fudged" our scores. In two or three days the entire class had qualified.

Back at the base we met with a group of tailors from Los Angeles who measured us for our new officer uniforms. The army gave us an allowance of $300.00 to purchase these. I

...I had been awarded a Good Conduct Medal, and now I had a red ribbon to wear on my otherwise drab uniform. As a rule, the cadets were a very well behaved bunch of guys. We realized we had better watch our steps because the Army would not put up with any foolishness. We had a lot to lose. We all wanted those wings and commissions, and nobody wanted to "wash out" due to bad behavior. Even today, I believe those cadets were the greatest group of young men I have ever known.

spent $250.00 that day for my blouse, cap, four pairs of pants, three wool shirts, two khaki shirts, a raincoat, belt, and all the cap and blouse ornamentation.

The last week before graduation was exceptionally busy. A full day was devoted to an extremely rigid physical exam. I had my photograph made, I made my will, and signed a hundred forms. The army had a $10,000 life insurance policy on me as a cadet but if I wanted to retain it, I now had to begin to pay the premiums. I chose to purchase it and was glad Uncle Sam did not ever have to pay it out.

I took one last ride with the squadron bombardier. I had come close to the shack many times before, but this day, out of the five bombs, I hit the thing dead center two times. The instructor went hog wild, yelled, and even hugged me.

Next to last day, my new ID card was made. I got my last cadet pay and I borrowed $150 from the Bank of America to buy a train ticket home to Virginia.

02 October 1943, a Saturday, was graduation day. Our uniforms had arrived, and we were allowed to put them on, and the latrine was a mad house, with everyone trying to get in front of a mirror to admire himself. Mine was a perfect fit and was I ever proud. I had never owned such a nice set of "threads." I felt the tailoring company had done a superb job.

Approximately 15% of my class had "washed out" during the three months at Victorville but that was a great deal better than the two-thirds of my pilot class at Decatur that did not make it. At the last minute, we learned that some of the class would not be commissioned second lieutenants but would be given the rank of flight officer. This was a recent development and this rank was on par with a warrant officer. It was somewhere between an enlisted man and a commissioned officer. The shoulder insignia was a blue enameled bar. Their pay was the same as a second lieutenant.

The ceremonies were held in the post theatre with ninety-eight cadets receiving wings and new ranks. There were pitifully few family members present and the whole thing went off without much fanfare and did not take very long. The band played, and we walked across the stage twice, once to be commissioned, and once to receive the bombardier wings, and that was it.

Outside we were mobbed by a horde of enlisted men. The army had a tradition that an officer gave a dollar to the first GI who saluted him, so all these soldiers were shoving and

My first photo as a lieutenant

My parents had this photo of me taken while I was at home in Lexington in October 1943.

pushing with one hand in a salute and the other out for his dollar.

I was given an honorable discharge from the Aviation Cadet Program and a new officer serial number. My new number was 0-756941. My new orders were to report to the air base in Salt Lake City with a 10-day delay en route.

(I have names of 33 of my classmates who were killed in action or became prisoners of war before VJ day. I doubt that half of my class came through the war unscathed).

I hated to leave Victorville. I really enjoyed this place and the instruction. It was so much

Honorable Discharge
from
The Army of the United States

TO ALL WHOM IT MAY CONCERN:

This is to Certify, That* ARTHUR W. ORDEL, JR.

† 13062784, AVIATION CADET, FROV AVIATION CADET DETACHMENT, VAAF, VICTORVILLE, CALIF

THE ARMY OF THE UNITED STATES, as a TESTIMONIAL OF HONEST AND FAITHFUL SERVICE, is hereby HONORABLY DISCHARGED from the military service of the UNITED STATES by reason of ‡ CONVENIENCE OF GOVERNMENT SECT X AR 615-360 TO ACCEPT COMMISSION AUS

Said ARTHUR W. ORDEL, JR. was born in MILTON, in the State of PENNSYLVANIA

When enlisted he was 20 years of age and by occupation a STUDENT

He had BLUE eyes, BROWN hair, RUDDY complexion, and was FIVE feet NINE & ONE HALF inches in height.

Given under my hand at VICTORVILLE ARMY AIR FIELD, VICTORVILLE, CALIF this 1ST day of OCTOBER, one thousand nine hundred and FORTY THREE.

EARL C. ROBBINS, Colonel, Air Corps
Commandant

Commanding.

See AR 340-470.
*Insert name; as, "John J. Doe."
†Insert Army serial number, grade, company, regiment or arm or service as "1620032", "Corporal, Company A, 1st Infantry"; "Sergeant, Quartermaster Corps."
‡If discharged prior to expiration of service, give number, date, and source of order or full description of authority therefor.   16-19969

W. D., A. G. O. Form No. 55
October 6, 1939

better than my two years of college. One thing I did not appreciate until later was that, as an officer, I would never have as good food or better living quarters than I had as an aviation cadet.

I spent graduation afternoon packing my belongings, saying goodbyes, and preparing to leave. That evening at the mess hall we were treated to an outstanding farewell dinner of steak with all the trimmings.

Sunday morning I caught the train for Virginia, starting my life of a brand-new second lieutenant. On the train I began to reminiscence upon the momentous past year. Last October I entered the service, green as grass, and having absolutely no idea of what was ahead for me. Now here I was a second lieutenant in the Army Air Corps with silver wings above my left pocket. Each day had

In uniform with my father and brother, Ron, in Lexington, VA, 1941

been an adventure, and new experiences came almost hourly. I thought of all the testing at Nashville, the high altitude tank, the poison gas tent at Maxwell field, solo flying at Decatur, and the cross-country train ride to California, how nice Santa Ana was, and the thrill of bombing the desert at Victorville. How many people had been fortunate enough to experience all these things in one year, at the age of twenty-two? I was pretty pleased with myself.

My folks had moved to Lexington, Virginia, since my last visit. My four-day train ride ended in Staunton, Virginia, where my folks were waiting to drive me home. This visit was much happier than the last one but I realized my parents were still very apprehensive

Sunday morning I caught the train for Virginia, starting my life of a brand-new second lieutenant. On the train I began to reminiscence upon the momentous past year. Last October I entered the service, green as grass, and having absolutely no idea of what was ahead for me.

regarding my future. While Lexington was a nice little town, I knew no one and I felt a complete stranger. Before I knew it, I was on a train bound for Salt Lake, Utah. I spent seven days of the ten-day leave riding the train.

PERSONNEL ORDERS)

No.   50)

HEADQUARTERS
ARMY AIR FORCES WESTERN FLYING TRAINING COMMAND
1104 West 8th Street, Santa Ana, California
2 October 1943

EXTRACT

* i * * *

8. Pursuant to authority contained in Paragraph 2, sub-Paragraph 3, Army Regulation 35-1480, 10 October 1942, and TWX TE 274 J, Headquarters, AAF Flying Training Command, 6 October 1942, the following-named Second Lieutenants, Army of the United States (Air Corps), graduates of Class WFTC 43-14, AAF Bombardier School, Victorville Army Air Field, Victorville, California, each of whom holds an aeronautical rating, are hereby required to participate in regular and frequent aerial flights.

Glen Woodrow Adams	Clarence Franks, Jr.	Selma Lee McDougle	Joseph Cleveland Stallard
Raleigh Lynwood Alderson	Frederick Blair Fults	Charles Joseph O'Brien	Fred Mack Standley
Robert Lewis Alford	Harry F Gerloff	Arthur William Ordel, Jr.	Albert Earl Steelhammer
Thomas George Anas	Clinton Winfield Gibler	Rute Hugh Parrilla	Darell Lee Stevens
Rito Fuentes Arellano	Ralph Garland Gillham	Gilbert Lale Payne	William Donald Stevens
Jeffrey Francis Babin	Jim Box Goodner, Jr.	Raymond Donald Penhall	Ray Leon Stewart
Lowell Dean Baker	James Clayton Gramling	Lewis Sevier Peters	Orville Zellen Stocker, Jr.
Arthur Robert Barbiers, Jr.	Jack Graves	Preston George Philhower	Joseph Claude Stricker
Herbert Earl Bayer	Charles Curtis Harper, Jr.	Donald Edward Pior	Edward Joseph Struewing, Jr.
J W Boten	William Parker Hays	Roy Charles Plog	Richard Takvorian
Ralph Bothe	John William Heck	Harold Robert Reeves	Linder Tanksley
Ralph Jean Bradbury	Carl Abbott Herrmann	John Christopher Reichardt	David Lotus Taylor
Vernon Oscar Breazeale	Alton Shelby Hill	Melvin Jay Rich	Charles Robert Terpening
James Joseph Brooks	Eddie Franklin Hinson, Jr.	Jack Leischow Rider	Roy Estel Thompson
Frederick Anson Brown, III	Thomas Ivey	David Ririe	William Edward Thompson
John Ellsworth Brown	Asahel Glen Kellogg	Jacob Dennard Rives	Weyman James Tow
Paul Frederick Burton	Thomas Christopher Kerins	Clarence James Ross	George Louis Turcott, Jr.
Arthur Thomas Caine	James Robert Kline	Walter Franklin Ross	Earl Wilbert Turner
McKinnon Cameron	Gerald Vernon Krauss	Harold Morris Scherr	Thomas Joseph Upmeier
William James Champ	Kenneth Richard Lincoln	Lewis Milton Raymond Scott	Daniel A Walton
James Harvey Chance	Benjamin Kelly Lohman	William Clement Scott	Richard Kendrick Ware
Dempse Hearn Curry	Dana Wiley Maryott	Richard Franklin Sherman	Gavin Watson, Jr.
C W Lesley Dennis	Jack Milton Michaelson	Albert Elmo Silva	Henry Lee Wilson, Jr.
John Houston Doherty	Herbert Julius Moschach	James William Snyder	Owen Walter Womack
Paul Easley Foster	John George McAllister		

All orders in conflict with this order are revoked.

* * * *

By Command of Major General COUSINS:

OFFICIAL:

L. A. WALTON,
Brigadier General, GSC,
Chief of Staff

T. R. HORNADAY,
Colonel, AGD,
Adjutant General

This order made me a Second Lieutenant and a Bombardier.

CHAPTER 7

Crew Training On The B-17

Salt Lake City, Utah
1943 October

My arrival in Salt Lake City was unceremonious. "Second Looies" were pouring into town by the trainloads. I had the feeling that nobody knew what to do with all of us. I ran into a couple of my Victorville classmates and we checked into a hotel for a few days before reporting for duty. One of these was McKinnon Cameron, a red-headed Scotsman who had been a friend in bombardier school. I was mighty happy to see him again. When we finally checked in, we were assigned to The Cattle Exhibition Building at the Utah State Fair Grounds. We were told there would be five hundred of us each morning for an out-of-door roll call.

The weather turned extremely cold and snowy. Most of the guys did not have warm coats and there were absolutely no overcoats available for purchase in any store. The best to be found was some type of raincoat. While I was on leave in Lexington, Virginia, I was fortunate enough to have found an overcoat at the shop which supplied uniforms to the military personnel at VMI. It was a beautiful coat of heavy wool fabric with the finest tailoring. The price tag was $50.00. My Dad was horrified when he found I had "blown that much on a coat." I do not believe an Ordel had ever owned a $50.00 coat. That coat treated me well in Salt Lake City, during the rest of my army life, and for many years after. In fact, my son, Bill, even wore it while he was in high school.

The military finally began to get their act together. After two weeks in the "Cattle Barn" we moved to an adjunct to the main army base. Strangely enough, we were not permitted on the main base. Our barracks were brand new and just like the ones in Nashville. Heat was supplied by two coal stoves and we were supposed to maintain the fires ourselves. Most of the time we were in town and when we returned the fires were out and the building was frigid.

The 8:00 a.m. roll call continued and they began to round us up for classes, lectures, and even some drilling. We did not take kindly to the marching up and down when we could be in town goofing off. I began to realize there was much friction between the tactical (ground) officers and the officers who wore wings. These tactical officers fed us, doctored us, paid us, kept track of us, and generally administered to us. Many were ROTC graduates or had received their commissions at an OCS (Officer Candidate School). We called them ninety-day wonders or ground grippers. I do not know what they called us, but they let it be known that they thought we were undisciplined, unmilitary, and out of control.

I got my first pay as a second lieutenant at the end of October. The pay was $150.00 a month, plus $75.00 a month flight pay. Of course, there were the usual deductions for insurance, my debt to VPI, and my loan from the Bank of America. The remaining money was issued in cash and I recall feeling pretty wealthy. After being in Salt Lake City for six or so weeks, at roll call one morning, I found I had been assigned to a combat crew and ordered to report to Ardmore, Oklahoma, for additional training. The orders listed the crew as pilot, Lt. Robert Gilmore from Wisconsin; co-pilot, Lt. Charles N. Baker from California; waist gunner, Sgt. Charles Wittleder from Chicago; crew chief and top turret gunner, Sgt. Robert Bucky Walters from Long Island; and me as bombardier. The five of us were to be the nucleus of the ten-man crew #862 U.S. Army Air Corps.

Ardmore, Oklahoma
Actual B-17 Training Begins

It was a two day ride on a "troop train" to Ardmore, Oklahoma. The only thing I remember about the journey was eating Thanksgiving dinner in the dining car enroute. I later learned the other members of the new crew were on the same train, however, we did not meet until we arrived at Ardmore. I have no recollection of the first meeting with my crew, but it must have been the day we arrived or the day after. We were

Bob Gilmore, our pilot and stalwart crew commander

Left to Right: Officers of Crew #862 Bob Gilmore, Bob Munroe, Art Ordel, and Charles Baker

joined by navigator Lt. Robert Munroe from Kansas; radio operator Sgt. Milbert (Jerry) Maisch from South Dakota; and ball turret gunner, Sgt. Fred Anderson, a Texan. A week or so later tail gunner Sgt. Tom Coburn from Tennessee joined us. The nine of us quickly grew into a close-knit crew as we trained together for the next three months.

Ardmore was a non-descript place, just a few miles north of the Texas line and very close to the famous cowboy actor Gene Autry's ranch. The air base was DISMAL and the weather was no better.

We were pleased to learn we would be flying the famed B-17, "Flying Fortress." Lt. Robert Gilmore had earlier pilot training in a B-17 school, but the rest of us had never even been in one. I was awed by the size of this plane and the roominess of the nose, which was to become my "office." (All the planes were [F] models and none had mounts for machine guns in the nose, though there was plenty of space). I can remember only one ride with a bombardier instructor who spent the time talking about the various switches and controls on the bombardier's instrument panel, the bomb bay, and how the bomb bay doors operated. He never once mentioned the Norden bombsight, so I supposed he thought I knew all about

We were pleased to learn we would be flying the famed B-17, "Flying Fortress." Lt. Robert Gilmore had earlier pilot training in a B-17 school, but the rest of us had never even been in one. I was awed by the size of this plane and the roominess of the nose, which was to become my "office."

B-17s over Ardmore, Oklahoma, in December 1943

it. We flew two or three active bombing missions, including one at night. We dropped the same one-hundred-pound bombs we had used in Victorville.

The chief of the bombardier training section was 1st Lt. Kermit Beehan, who had seen action in North Africa and was extremely nervous. I thought for his own good he would have been better off in civilian life. We flew a couple of navigation missions but the main emphasis was on piloting and the rest of us just were there for the ride.

Ardmore Army Air Base was no Garden of Eden but I do not remember any gripes or complaints. We four officers were squeezed into a small room furnished with two wooden double deck beds and nothing else. We had been issued B-4 Valpak hanging bags and these substituted for clothes closets. Everything else was either on the floor or hung on nails driven into the wooden wall. All plumbing was a short walk to another building. We got well acquainted with each other and we four officers began to become really close friends.

Bob Gilmore, age 25, was the oldest, with a BS degree in agriculture and had taught school for a year before entering the Aviation Cadet Training Program.

Chuck Baker, age 24, had been a student at Oregon State University where he majored in physical education and music. He also played football and the cello. He had been drafted into the cavalry, played football, and boxed for the Army at Fort Riley, Kansas. He went to the aviation cadets, received pilot wings, and expected to train for P-38 fighter planes, but was made a co-pilot of a B-17. He was crushed since this was the equivalent of training for the Indy 500 but instead being assigned to the right-hand seat of dump truck.

Bob Munroe, 23, was married and had been to pilot school. He washed out late in training,

Unbeknownst to me, "Chuck" Baker made this likeness of me shortly after we arrived in Ardmore. I had no idea until he presented it to me.

There was no insulation between me and the outside world, just a thin layer of aluminum and some plexiglas. The wind-chill factor was rough on a nice day, but brutal on cold days. It was slightly better in the cockpit, since it had heat coming from the engines. The nose had no heat except what the sun furnished.

and he went on to earn navigator wings. He was planning to go to law school after the war.

I at 22, was the youngest officer. I weighed 152 lbs. and was 5 feet 11 inches tall.

Enlisted crew members were the following: Bucky Walters was 19 or 20 years old and said he was a race car driver before the war. He had been through mechanics and gunnery schools and now would man the plane's top turret. He was short, stocky, cheerful, and definitely the crew chief. Jerry Maisch was two months older than I, and had been raised on a farm in South Dakota. He was quiet, both in the air and on the ground, and I frequently didn't know he was around. He graduated from radio and gunnery schools and would man the radio and the machine gun which stuck out the roof. (I doubt he ever fired that gun.) Charles Wittleder had graduated from gunnery school. He was our turret expert, and he operated one of the waist guns and was a "mother hen type." Fred (Andy) Anderson was a thin, long, and lanky Texan, 19 or 20 years old. I think he came into the service right out of high school, was most likable, and I never understood how he squeezed himself into the ball turret since he was so tall. Tom Coburn was probably in his thirties and a true loner but perhaps being back in the tail gun position by himself made him that way. Fate threw us together and I have often marveled at how close and compatible we became.

The training at Ardmore was intensive and very serious. We flew everyday. I spent a lot of my time exploring the plane, to become familiar with the sys-

Art Ordel, Bob Gilmore, and Chuck Baker. We did not realize an Indian had "butted" in.

53

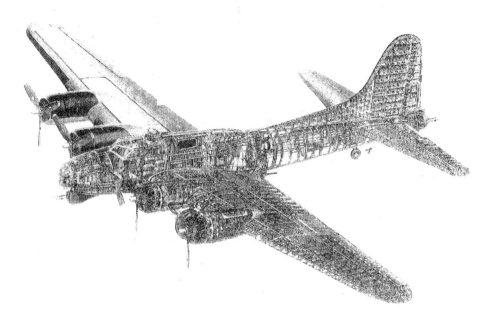

tems, and all gun positions. I particularly liked to ride in the ball turret, spinning it around, and waving the guns at my imaginary enemy. Hanging underneath the plane was an exciting sensation. The designers of the B-17 did not have much regard for comfort of the crew. Those four twelve-hundred-horsepower engines were so loud, one had to be beside someone to be heard. There was no insulation between me and the outside world, just a thin layer of aluminum and some plexiglas. The wind-chill factor was rough on a nice day, but brutal on cold days. It was slightly better in the cockpit, since it had heat coming from the engines. The nose had no heat except what the sun furnished. One glaring omission of the Boeing designers was no powder room. There was a high-tech device called a relief tube in the bomb bay. It consisted of a small funnel attached to a long piece of rubber tubing. Woe to the man who tried to use it when Gilmore was aware. Gillie would hit the switch which opened the bomb bay doors, played the rudder pedals and make the ship swing back and forth, leaving the person standing on a five-inch catwalk. Nothing between him and Mother

Flying at two hundred miles per hour in turbulent air with an instructor telling you to stick your wing into the other plane's window while watching all your instruments, took a lot of concentration. Sticking your wing into the other plane's propeller or letting him do it to you means you suddenly are wearing angel wings and playing a harp.

Earth except many thousand feet of air, he would be grabbing with both hands for something solid to hang on to. The desire to continue would suddenly vanish.

When we had no night training mission scheduled, we had the evening to ourselves. After going to town a couple of times, we decided there was more going on at the base than the town and stayed at the base and shot the bull. When the weather was bad and we could not fly, there was always ground school with lectures on all types of military subjects. Munroe and I had to return to code class, where we were obliged to increase our speed in sending and receiving Morse code. 1943 Christmas came and went and I have no recollection of the day. We probably had to fly.

Shortly after Christmas, my mother wrote she was coming to Ardmore to see me. She had been very depressed since the death of my brother Bob and thought the trip might help her. She had a tiring three-day bus ride from Virginia to Oklahoma and was thoroughly worn out when she arrived at the hotel. She planned to stay only two or three days.

My mother, Jessie Welliver Ordel and I in downtown Ardmore, Oklahoma, December 1943

Somehow she met a schoolteacher, who had an extra room, so she stayed on for two weeks. My mother had not known any of Bob's shipmates on the *Maddox* which went down. She was quite anxious to meet my crew. She brought with her white silk scarves, which she had sewn, for each of the officers to wear while flying. Each one of us still had his when we met at reunions after the war. Because of my tight schedule, I could not see her every day but she was feeling better by the time she returned to Virginia.

One weekend in January, Munroe made arrangements for us to go to Wichita. We got leave and took the train that headed for his hometown, Augusta, Kansas. We met his family, ate some Kansas home cooking, saw the sights, and had a most agreeable two days in the big city.

I never thought flying a four-engine bomber was a joy ride. It was inherently dangerous and hard work for the two pilots. Having had more experience would also have been preferable. Formation flying was particularly hazardous. Flying at two hundred miles per hour in turbulent air with an instructor telling you to stick your wing into the other plane's window while watching all your instruments, took a lot of concentration. Sticking your wing into the other plane's propeller or letting him do it to you means you suddenly are wearing angel wings and playing a harp.

I never gave any thought to the perils we faced. We certainly never talked about it. We saw all the war movies but I had a detached view of the whole business. John Wayne and Errol Flynn and other film heroes might have gotten banged up a bit, but it was always just a flesh wound. They always had a gorgeous nurse to take care of them. The good guys always won. The only people killed were Nazis or Japs. On occasion we would be faced with the reality. Two of my Victorville classmates were killed in separate plane crashes at Ardmore.

One day was devoted to a gunnery mission. We flew down to Galveston, Texas, and were briefed for this.

We took off again flying out over the Gulf of Mexico. Our target was a "sleeve" towed by a B-26. Each of us was allowed a short burst from the waist gun which was loaded with tracer bullets, so we could see where they were going. That was the first time I had fired a machine gun from a moving plane. The next time was at a Messerschmitt over Germany. Flying back to Ardmore from Galveston, Gilmore hit the bail-out button. I was up in the nose when I

Art Ordel and Charles Baker, each shown in front of their Ardmore barracks. "The barracks were as rough inside as on the outside."

heard it, but my parachute was not there. After a mad scramble to the back of the plane, I found it swinging from one of the waist guns. Gilmore had sounded the alarm by mistake. I learned a lesson and I never lost sight of my "chute" again.

Our training at Ardmore was coming to an end. We thought we knew it all and we were full of confidence. We didn't know if we were going to war in the Atlantic or the Pacific but we were ready and willing to get on with it. The last memorable event at Ardmore started in, of all places, code class.

Munroe and I were in this class which met two or three days a week at 5 a.m. If one want-

We thought we knew it all and we were full of confidence. We didn't know if we were going to war in the Atlantic or the Pacific but we were ready and willing to get on with it.

ed breakfast before class, it meant getting up very early on a cold January day in Oklahoma. It started out that way, and then we started skipping breakfast. A lot of us began to skip roll call. The instructor was a warrant officer and the class consisted of over a hundred bombardiers and navigators. One morning the roll call instructor noticed that only a dozen or so seats were occupied. He called the roll a second time, and that list of absentees was sent to the base commander. The colonel sent each one of the goof-offs a Reply By Endorsement (RBI), which required one to return the form with a written explanation of the absence. A corporal in Headquarters who had typed up the RBIs, let the word out that he had not kept a list of the men receiving them and we probably could ignore them. Most of us did,

but Munroe's wife, Gerry, had come to Ardmore to spend this last week with him, and he had been going into town each night to see her. Bob was afraid he would be confined to the base if he did not reply. He concocted some sort of alibi and returned it to the colonel. He was promptly confined to the base for the duration of the time there. The rest of us got no punishment at all. Bob stayed at the base the first night, but the next, he said he didn't care what they did to him; he was going into town to be with Gerry. Later that evening we were in our cozy

Left to right: Ordel, Munroe, Gilmore, and Baker, Ardmore, Oklahoma

Bob Munroe and wife Gerry

quarters when a second lieutenant, accompanied by a mean looking MP (Military Police) came in. The lieutenant said he was Officer of the Day and he was looking for Munroe. I said "I think he is at the Officer's Club." He left and half an hour later he returned saying he had looked all over the Officer's Club and Munroe was not there. I said, "You just missed him—he went to the Post Exchange." They left, and soon returned, saying he was not there. I said he had gone to take a shower. They soon returned saying he was not there. I do not know what got into me but I stood up and said "You little x~#*#+x. Munroe has gone to town to see his wife and if you report this, I'm going to knock the (you know what) out of you. They backed out, Bob continued going to town, and we did not see that dynamic duo again while at Ardmore. Stay tuned for the rest of the story....

A day or two before we left Ardmore, a tenth

Crew 862, Ardmore, Oklahoma, February 1944
Back L-R: Robert Walters, Top Turret; Jimmy Stewart, Waist Gunner; Jerry Maisch, Radioman; Fred Anderson, Ball Turret; Charles Wittleder, Waist Gunner; Tom Coburn, Tail Gunner. Front, L-R: Bob Gilmore, Pilot; Bob Munroe, Navigator; Art Ordel, Bombardier; Chuck Baker, co-pilot, missing due to illness

man, the other waist gunner, was added to the crew. He moved into the barracks with our gunners, and I went over to meet him. His name was Jimmy Stewart (not the famous actor) and had been a line mechanic stationed at Ardmore for two years. He looked old enough to be my father. I asked him where he had gone to gunnery school and he said he had not. I said, "But you are wearing gunner's wings," and he said it is a long story. Jimmy Stewart was from Mississippi and had married a very young girl in order to put her through high school. He would get homesick for her, and if they failed to give him a pass to go home, he would just walk out, and hitchhike home. He would come back in a couple of days. He had done this several times. In fact, he had just come back two days before. The day before, the provost marshal had come to his cell, handed him some corporal stripes, and a pair of gunner's wings. He said, "Jimmy, put these on your uniform because I'm sending you to where you can't hitch-hike back to Mississippi every time you feel like it." So we inherited him. I am not sure he ever fired his guns over Germany but he knew more about the innards of a B-17 than any of us, and I considered him a valuable crew member. He was a mild mannered Southerner who enjoyed a drink, but was a handful when he had a few too many.

Two or three days before our departure from this base, the Army made a photo of our crew. Unfortunately, Baker was in the hospital with tonsillitis and missed this event.

28 February

The time to move on from Ardmore had arrived. I was eager for our next adventure. I would look back at this place with absolutely no regrets. I had no warm thoughts of this base and was optimistic that our next station would be more hospitable.

Restless
to Begin

CHAPTER 8

Across The North Atlantic

28 February, 1944

We left Ardmore, Oklahoma, on the train very early, and later the same day arrived by train at the air base at Grand Island, Nebraska. I do not remember much about the move. Grand Island was a staging area, the army's name for a place from which crews went overseas. We did not know which direction we were going to be sent until we each opened a package to reveal a machete, a compass, a fishing line, and various jungle survival gear. There was a place for a pistol but the weapon was missing. We guessed that we would be bombing Tokyo.

We waited a week for the wind to stop blowing. When it did, we were taken to the flight line and issued a brand new, very shiny B-17 airplane. What a thrill! We now had our own plane and we began discussing a name for it. The following day we gave it a thorough flight check and calibrated the compass, and the jungle gear was turned back in.

At last, final travel orders were cut for the trip. We were routed to Goose Bay, Labrador, via Presque Isle, Maine, and on to Iceland, England, and the Eighth Air Force. I was thrilled when I realized we would be playing in the Big League. Eagerly we packed all our belongings, went to bed to be awakened early. We took off on the 10th of March at 5:00 a.m.

Under way, Gilmore announced he was going to take a small detour and give his hometown, Cambria, Wisconsin, a "buzz job." We arrived there about 8:00 just when that little town was coming to life. We tore down the main street at about 10 feet altitude. I looked up and saw the two-story buildings higher than we were. He made a couple more passes, circled the farm where he had lived, and proceeded to Maine.

A month after we arrived in England, Gillie received a package from Cambria, Wisconsin, full of letters from school kids and newspaper clippings, telling about their exciting morning. Evidently, this was the greatest thing that ever happened to that little town.

I asked Gillie to detour over Niagara Falls but he said we had already wasted too much time and he couldn't do it. I was very put out because I had never been to Niagara Falls and this might be my last chance. The rest of the flight was uneventful until we landed at Presque Isle, Maine. While taxiing, a strong gust of wind caught our tall tail and swung the plane into a snow bank, damaging the tail surfaces.

I am surprised that no one questioned our ten-hour flight that should have taken a few hours less than that.

We were stranded in Maine until repairs could be completed but nobody complained. There were ample recreational facilities and the one that most appealed to me was ice skating. A plane hangar had been flooded with a couple inches of water, which became solid ice, and skates were available for the asking. It was cold as the devil outside, but inside, out of the wind, it was quite cozy and lots of fun.

One evening we visited the "Hotel De Gink," an eating place where transatlantic travelers could get a beef steak, the last one before leaving the States. Our young waitress was gaga over us when we told her we were flying across the Atlantic to Europe to fight Hitler and the Nazis, and we would love to have her give us something personal to carry, for good luck. She

These flight reports had to be signed by staff Sergeant Walters to verify their accuracy.

went into the ladies' room and in a minute or so she came out with a big lock of hair which she had cut from her head and tied in a ribbon. We thanked her profusely and trashed it when we got back to the barracks.

The day before we left, each of the crew members was presented with a denim bag containing a deck of cards, a paperback book, some toilet articles, a pair of dice and some snacks. These gifts were provided by the good citizens of Presque Isle, to all the air crews going over seas. This was not unusual as the military in this era was solidly supported by the American people. I still have my bag.

15 March we left the US following the St. Lawrence River and the Gaspé Peninsula, to Goose Bay, Labrador. This was not a scenic trip. The land was not hospitable and all one could see was snow and frozen lakes. The air base at Goose Bay was easy to spot in the snow since the runway had been sprinkled with red sand. The base was occupied jointly by the US Army and the Royal Canadian Air Force. We were on one side and they were on the other side. Snow was on the ground when we left Ardmore, more snow at Grand Island, more and deeper snow at Presque Isle. Here the snow had drifted to the top of the two-story buildings. The cold was very penetrating. A line mechanic told us that if one threw a bucket of gasoline into the air, none of it would reach the ground because it would evaporate in the frigid air.

The second day was spent briefing for the flight next day. We would be crossing the North Atlantic and arrive at Meeks Field, Iceland. Incidentally, this was my first time ever out of the good ole' USA. That night before going to bed we watched the Aurora Borealis (Northern Lights). What a spectacular sight.

On March 17 we were awakened at some horrible hour, and fed a good and hearty breakfast since no food would be served on this next flight. They told us our Group of fifty planes would be the first to fly the northern route to Europe at this time of year. We would fly singly; no follow-the-leader. I remember it was just seventeen years before that Charles Lindbergh had made his historic flight across the Atlantic, but that had been in May, and much further south. He got his name and pictures in all the newspapers, but we did not.

Final instructions were received and the weather was predicted to be unusually good. The flight plan was to fly to Greenland, turn right, and continue on to Iceland. With tongue in cheek we were also told, if something goes wrong, don't worry, you won't last a half an hour in that frigid water. There would be no rescue squads, and the lack of navigation systems in this part of the world at this time was unbelievable.

We took off, and had hardly gotten the wheels up before we hit a blinding snow storm. We climbed and soon put on oxygen masks, so we could climb to 20,000 feet before we were

The flight plan was to fly to Greenland, turn right, and continue on to Iceland. With tongue in cheek we were also told, if something goes wrong, don't worry, you won't last a half an hour in that frigid water. There would be no rescue squads, and the lack of navigation systems in this part of the world at this time was unbelievable.

in the clear. Gilmore asked Munroe the navigator where we were, and Bob reported "I don't know, but I'll get my octant out and take a shot on the sun, and get us located." He stuck his head up in the astrodome, and all he could see was a thick coating of ice on the plexiglas.

We continued flying using "dead reckoning" but soon Gilmore found the radio signal from Cape Prince Christian on Greenland's south coast, and he took a bearing on it. The clouds broke up as we approached land, and Munroe could fine-tune his navigating. We could see land, but we turned before we got over it. He pointed our location, corrected the bearings, and we continued on the journey.

During this flight the gunners and I had nothing to do, except slowly freeze to death. The thermometer was sitting on forty-two degrees below zero Celsius. The wind chill factor was off the chart (as if we had had a chart). I was so cold that I didn't care if we never got to

...We hit a blinding snow storm. We climbed and soon put on oxygen masks, so we could climb to 20,000 feet before we were in the clear. Gilmore asked Munroe the navigator where we were, and Bob reported "I don't know, but I'll get my octant out and take a shot on the sun, and get us located." He stuck his head up in the astrodome, and all he could see was a thick coating of ice on the plexiglas.

Iceland. I decided to go to the back of the plane to see how the enlisted men were faring, and when I opened the door between the bomb bay and the radio room, I saw all six of them huddled on the floor passing around an electric gun heater which was a metal U-shaped device which fitted over the top and sides of a .50-caliber machine gun to prevent it from freezing. The men had their shoes off, and were taking turns putting their feet on this device to warm them up. I was invited to join this tootsie toasting party, and needless to say, happily squeezed into the circle.

The weather cleared. We descended to the point where it was possible to take off oxygen masks. It became warmer so I went back to the nose to watch for Iceland, but the weather turned bad and we were in the fog again. As we neared Iceland we continued to descend, and Munroe called Gilmore for our altitude. Gillie said 500 feet and Munroe said, "Umm, according to my charts, the mountains here go up to 1500 feet." Scary!

The tower and our pilots then made radio contact and were directed to the field. We descended and finally broke into the clear. As we started to land, we could see we were on a collision course with a B-24 which would be landing on our runway from the opposite direction. The tower operators screamed at him and he pulled up, went around, and landed behind us. The poor guy was about out of gas and desperate to get onto land. Our arrival in Iceland was more exciting than I wished and I was mighty glad to get my feet on solid ice and snow.

I saw all six of them huddled on the floor passing around an electric gun heater which was a metal U-shaped device which fitted over the top and sides of a .50-caliber machine gun to prevent it from freezing. The men had their shoes off, and were taking turns putting their feet on this device to warm them up.

We were billeted that night in a Quonset hut. The floor was a foot or so below ground level, and each time someone came in he shook off snow which left the floor in an inch of water.

The term jet-lag had not yet been coined, but I know I was dead tired. I suppose I had a meal and then went to bed, but I cannot recall doing either. Next morning when I went to brush my teeth, I discovered my toothpaste had frozen solid, split the tube, melted, and liquid was spread all over my gear. One of our gunners had brought along a bushel of oranges, but when he checked them, they had frozen, turned black, and were rotting. He had planned to sell them in England at a big profit. So much for American capitalism.

The weather here was awful. One minute it was clear, and the next minute a howling blizzard would be raging. When outside, I could barely see my hand in front of my face. The snow never came down, but blew sideways at a hundred miles an hour. I was hoping to see something of Iceland, but alas, all I saw was snow, ice and fog.

We only stayed one night in Keflavik, and resumed flight the next morning, heading for Stornoway in the Outer Hebrides, off the northwest coast of Scotland. I stayed in the nose on this part of our trip. Visibility on this leg of the journey was poor, and the pilots flew most of the leg on instruments. The air was exceedingly turbulent, and I couldn't see beyond the ends of the wings. I had an eerie feeling that they were waving good-bye to me. We ran through rain, and with all that plexiglas around me I had the sensation of being in a submarine.

Stornoway was solidly "socked in" when we arrived. We circled for an hour or so and then were diverted to Prestwick, Scotland. Again we circled for an hour, before finally we were let down to land. We broke out of the clouds to see the most wonderfully, green pastoral world I had ever laid eyes on. After a month of snow and more snow, this scene was truly beautiful.

Upon landing, we were told to remove all personal belongings, as we were being relieved of our airplane! What a disappointment! After bringing us all the way from Grand Island,

---

Stornoway was solidly "socked in" when we arrived. We circled for an hour or so and then were diverted to Prestwick, Scotland. Again we circled for an hour, before finally we were let down to land. We broke out of the clouds to see the most wonderfully, green pastoral world I had ever laid eyes on. After a month of snow and more snow, this scene was truly beautiful.

Nebraska, USA, to Prestwick, Scotland, without a whimper or a hiccup, we were losing her.

As we walked away it suddenly came to me that I was part of a very great crew. It had been a grueling trip with the pilots, navigator, and radio operator showing great skill and without one complaint or gripe expressed by anyone.

The Eighth Air Force had lost many crews along with their aircraft, and the B-17s were badly needed. Our plane would be assigned to a crew who came across on a troop ship.

I have often wondered how many of the crews who started this massive crossing were able to complete their journey. The pilots, the navigators, the radio operators, were pretty green. Our navigator, Bob Munroe from Kansas, probably never saw a body of water larger than a bathtub, and here he was, guiding us across the worst possible territory on the globe. Take the B-24 crew who almost ran over us coming into Iceland. A B-24 had a much larger fuel capacity than a B-17and he may have wandered all over the northern hemisphere before he finally made his landing at Meeks Field.

I have never seen in print the number of crews who failed to arrive at the European Theater of Operations. I believe that it would be shocking.

As we walked away it suddenly came to me that I was part of a very great crew. It had been a grueling trip with the pilots, navigator, and radio operator showing great skill and without one complaint or gripe expressed by anyone.

CHAPTER 9

Preparing For Combat

The United Kingdom

18 March 1944

In Scotland we were trucked to the Adamton House, a picturesque, very British manor house on a large estate. We cleaned up, put on dress uniforms, and dined on a very nice meal. I was tired and decided to hit the sack, but we heard music downstairs, and went to check it out and discovered a St. Patrick's Day party in progress. It was 18 March and the orchestra was playing Dipsy Doodle, a song that was popular in the USA while I was in high school. Not only were they a day late with their party, but they were several years late with the music. I went back upstairs, and went to bed.

Our stay in Prestwick was enjoyable, and all too brief. Next morning we boarded a compartment train and headed south toward England. It was a long ride and we did not arrive until after dark, but we enjoyed the ride, the rest, and the rural scenery. We had been given some "C" rations for meals as there were no dining facilities in the train. Our conductor volunteered to take our cans of food forward to the engine to be heated. We ate the heated part, and gave him the cold half, which included some cigarettes, a piece of chocolate, a bit of cheese, chewing gum, toilet paper, and some other stuff. He was most appreciative and told us a lot about London, where he lived, and about his young daughter who had had her hands injured in an air raid.

Our destination was Stone, UK, the 8th Air Force reception base where we were to spend four days. Although we had no duties, we were on shipping orders, which meant we were confined to the base, so we slept. We did slip out several times to visit a pub, and acquaint ourselves with the room-temperature British beer. I have no other recollections of this place.

25 March found us back on the train heading for Bovingdon, a base a short distance north of London, where we would attend flight school for two weeks.

There was some excitement our first night. About midnight, the Luftwaffe (German Air

Force) conducted a fifteen-minute bombing raid over London. We could hear the bombs exploding, and the anti-aircraft guns firing, and watched the many search lights in action, crisscrossing the sky.

Bovingdon was a British base, and so was the food. The only meat I remember was mutton and it was usually flavored with curry spice. It seemed to rain every day and the mud was deep everywhere.

Most of the instructors were veteran RAF (Royal Air Force) and their lectures were most interesting. One was given by an RAF officer who had interrogated German POWs. He gave us all his tricks to get information and said we could expect the same tactics to be used on us should we become prisoners of war. Another instructor, who had evaded capture after being shot down, gave us ideas on what to do in the event this happened to us. A commando taught us how to slit a throat or to stab from behind using a knee to push the blade in. We had been issued a dagger and sheath and I was ready to throw mine away. This man had seen action in North Africa and I believe he was talking from experience. I preferred to do my fighting from five miles up. We had eight hours of instruction daily and as I try to recall details, they almost run together.

They must have thought the bombardiers & gunners knew it all because most of the training was directed toward the pilots, navigator, and radio operator. We were restricted to the base, and didn't have a lot of free time, but we used what we had sleeping, playing cards, watching American movies, and discussing our next assignment.

We had arrived with only American money, and were able to exchange it on the base for British pounds, shillings, and pence. On the 31st, we got our first pay, and of course it was in this "funny money." There were slot machines along the food line in the mess hall, and naturally, we fed all our loose coins into these one-armed bandits.

06 April was the last day at Bovingdon. We learned we were assigned to the 390th Bomb Group located at Framlingham, East Anglia, northeast of Ipswich, and just a few miles inland from the North Sea. The 390th Group was commanded by Colonel Edgar Witten and had been awarded two Presidential Citations. We figured it must be a pretty hot outfit.

LAST MINUTE DETAILS
STATION
07 APRIL, 1944

We were awakened at 4:30 am. In true army style we waited until noon before we boarded the train to travel to Station. We were the very last to disembark.

It was late in the day when a GI truck met us, and delivered us to the base, about two miles away. Major Joe Gemmil, squadron commanding officer, and Major Bill Jones, executive officer welcomed us to the 570th Squadron. We ate supper, and were shown to our barracks.

The base was located approximately a two-hour train ride northeast of London in an area known as East Anglia. The region was overcrowded with American air bases. You could take off and immediately see three or four other airfields. That made flying in bad weather extremely dangerous. We were about six miles in from the North Sea, two or three miles from Framlingham Village, and the small village of Parham was at the very end of the runway.

The base had been built on a large estate, known as Moat Farm. It was a bucolic setting with dairy cows grazing in the fields adjacent to the barracks. The farm was owned by the Percy Kindrick family. The main house was constructed in the 17th century, and had a moat around it as protection from the Vikings, hence the name.

Our "digs" was a Quonset hut, complete with 20 cots, and a small coal-burning stove in the center. There were four empty cots at one end, which were to be ours. The sixteen current roommates said they were lucky cots, since the previous occupants had recently completed the required 25 missions, and returned to the US. (Within a month, each one of the 16 greeter men had been shot down outside the continent and listed as missing in action.) There were twenty men billeted here, the officers of five crews. The hut was very spartan with 20 tall clothes closets, made of heavy screen wire, and wooden slats, two dim light bulbs hanging from the ceiling. There were no chairs or tables.

The enlisted men were housed in a hut adjacent to the officer quarters which mirrored our quarters except there were 15 double bunk beds and they had a table with chairs for card playing. We each were provided two wool GI blankets, and a pillow. Instead of a mattress, we got three British "biscuits." These were about 30 x 30 inches and 2 or 3 inches thick. These were what we tried to sleep on. The cots had link springs, and every time one turned over, the biscuits would part and your butt ended up on the springs.

The next two weeks were busy ones, preparing for, in Chuck Baker's words, "doing battle with the Hun." We started right out with more ground school, covering such subjects as how to bail out of a crippled fort, first aid, using an oxygen mask, formation flying, ditching a B-17 into the sea, radio procedure, all conducted by experienced flyers. On the 13th, we took our first ETO (European Theater Operations) flight to practice formation flying. Tight formations were a necessity, as it massed our machine gun defense against the enemy fighters, and concentrated the falling bombs.

One evening, word came in that one of the crews in our barracks had been shot down. I was horrified to see some of our guys tearing apart their beds and grabbing any possession that looked comfortable. A couple of days later we lost another crew, and I was the first to grab a real mattress and two sheets from one of the beds. I slept much better after that. Those biscuits were a real pain in the back. My conscience was soothed later on, when I heard that the downed crew had made it safely into Switzerland and would remain there until the war ended.

During this period we were issued various pieces of flying gear, most of it new, but some of it obviously had seen some service. The nicest was a brand new flying jacket of olive green cloth with a fur collar, and a pile lining. It was a big improvement over the bulky leather sheepskin one I had been wearing. I was given two helmets, one a used sheepskin

Bombardier's flak suit has full armor. When he pulls ripcord at suit's center, entire suit falls off.

FLAK SUITS

I HAVE ON STREET CLOTHES, WOOL SWEATER, HEATED SUIT, COVERALLS,HEAVY PILE LINED FLYING JACKET, MAE WEST, PARACHUTE. OXYGEN MASK. GOGGLES, AND FLAK VEST

FLAK HELMETS

The flak helmet is personal issue. If you have worn both your flak suit and flak helmet on the mission, you have a good chance of returning the helmet to the supply room **personally** after the flight.

and another a steel helmet like the infantry wore. The sheepskin one had to have a hole cut to accommodate the earphones. By cutting just right, the headset would stay in place, and the wiring would attach to the part that stuck out of the hole. This did not take long, but the steel helmet was another matter. I had to make a crude flak helmet out of it by beating from the inside with a hammer to make it fit over the sheepskin one and the headset. It took me a couple of days pounding to make it fit and be comfortable.

I also got a throat microphone, which was worn around the neck with discs fitting on both sides of the Adams apple. I also received fur-lined boots, fur mittens, a Mae West, and a flak suit. The Mae West, named for the buxom film star of the 1930s, was an inflatable life jacket. It contained two chambers in the front, attached to CO_2 cylinders. A cord hung down from each side, and with one jerk of the cord, you had inflation, buoyancy, and figure enhancement. There was also a tube at the top with which one could inflate it by mouth, or deflate as needed.

The flak suit was a canvas garment that covered the back and chest, with a short skirt hanging down in the front. The darn thing was made of 2x2 inch squares of steel armor plate, sewn together and weighed some 30 pounds. It was quite cumbersome, and was supposed to make us bulletproof. I was also given an electric suit to keep me warm—a shiny, green two-piece pants and jacket that snapped together, with about four feet of cord to plug into the electrical system of the plane. I cannot remember what the pilots and Munroe got, but the gunners received a one piece bright blue quilted "Dr. Denton" type outfit. If the heat didn't work, they were thick enough to offer some warmth.

We were sent to the parachute shop to choose one of their offerings, and after a brief "show and tell," the pilots, Munroe, and the gunners were issued chest packs. This was a two-part outfit, a harness, and the removable chute, which was worn on the chest. It was awkward, but you could take the chute off, and keep it close by until needed. They showed me a backpack. It had a smaller canopy and meant I would come down faster, and land harder, but would always have it on and wouldn't have to look for it in an emergency. That is the one I elected. I weighed about 150 pounds at that time, and figured I wouldn't come down any harder than a 200-pound man in a large chute.

The pilots and Munroe were issued wrist watches, and in addition the pilots were given sunglasses. On a mission, if the plane got into real trouble, and they had to lighten the load so they could make it back to their base, they jettisoned the machine guns, all the ammo, the ball turret, and anything else that wasn't nailed down. If they made it back to the base, the pilots claimed they also had to throw their watches and glasses. I was not issued any goggles, but somewhere along the way, I acquired a pair of ski glasses, which I wore on all my missions, and eventually lost.

The Short Snorter
Prior to World War II almost no one had traveled by air across the Atlantic Ocean. The name came into use referring to a person who had made the flight and had their paper money autographed and taped into a long roll. Upon arrival at Stone Air Base UK, I eagerly made my Short Snorter.

We carried the photos of us wearing civilian clothes, that could be used for ID papers in the event we evaded capture. There was only one ensemble and all of us were pictured wearing it and years later, we learned that members of our Group who were shot down, were immediately identified as belonging to the 390th by that set of identical clothes.

One of the last things we got was a 45-caliber automatic pistol, complete with holster and two clips of ammo. I couldn't imagine trying to shoot my way out of Germany with that thing. Anyhow, I never carried it on a mission. I already had too much gear. When I put it all on, I could hardly stand up.

The 390th Bomb Group was formed at Geiger Field in Spokane Washington, in April 1943, and then moved to Orlando, Florida, and after a brief period of training it was posted to the Eighth Air Force in England. The first mission was to Bonn, Germany, on August 8th, 1943. In October, on a mission to Munster, eight B-17s were lost, and earned a Presidential Citation for shooting down or damaging 77 German planes. After the war ended, captured German records show that only 50 German planes were shot down that day, by all the American Forces.

All groups were identified in the air by a large white letter on a white square or a triangle painted on the plane's tail and wings. The 390th's insignia was a black "J" in a white square. A couple of nights after we arrived at the base we were awakened by a loud explosion, which we assumed to be a bomb. Next morning, we learned that it was a Pathfinder B-17 coming in to lead our Group on the day's mission. When he came in on final approach, a German night fighter, probably a ME-110, came up behind him, and shot him down. I was beginning to realize this war was for keeps, and one could get hurt in it. Another jolt came along when the Eighth Air Force decided to change combat policy, and required crews to complete 30 combat missions instead of 25. Our beloved General Jimmy Doolittle had ordered this change.

We continued to practice formation flying. Early in his tenure with the Eighth Air Force, General Curtis LeMay began to see the daylight bombing was not going well. The British had tried it, and went to night bombing only. They urged the US to do the same since losses of men and planes were just too great. General LeMay devised a formation in which the planes would fly very close to each other, and each would fly in a specified spot in the formation. This "combat box" was made up of three squadrons to form one group. There would be a lead squadron, a high squadron, slightly higher and behind on the right, a low squadron slightly below and behind on the left. There were six planes in each squadron, formed by two echelons of three planes each. Six planes in each squadron and three squadrons made up one group. No two planes in the group were at the same altitude, so that each one had a 360 degree field of fire and all eighteen planes could fire at the same enemy plane. At first, it was nerve wracking to be in such close proximity to another bomber, but soon it became comforting to be snuggled in with a dozen and a half friendly planes.

We had been at this Station two weeks, and were getting "antsy" about when we would be called up to take part in our first mission. Early in the morning of April 17, Munroe was called to fly with another crew. Bummer! I had a mixture of emotions about this, because we had been such a close team for six months. I was jealous, resentful, and mad, but still glad that it wasn't me flying with a strange crew. Gilmore and Baker must have felt the same, and after moping for a while, we decided to get some bikes, and pedal into Framlingham Village

British money with signatures

just to kill some time.

There was a 900-year-old castle located in the center of the village of Framlingham. That was our target for the afternoon. The castle's claim to fame was that Mary Queen of Scots (Bloody Mary) was staying there when she received word of her ascension to the throne. Baker had his camera, the weather was great, we scrambled around the castle, took a few pictures, and enjoyed a nice day in merrie olde England.

We returned to the base and sweated out Munroe's return.

Bob came back with a harrowing account of a mission to Oranienburg, a suburb of Berlin. The flak was fierce over the target and on the bomb run they were attacked by German fighter planes. Just as the bombardier released his bombs, he was hit by a piece of flak, just above the knee cap. The metal traveled up his thigh for about twelve inches. Bob was kept pretty busy, trying to put a bandage on, while firing his own guns. The guy had large thighs and Bob couldn't find a bandage big enough to go around the leg. After several tries, he tied several together. He got the bandage on, retrieved a morphine syrette from the first aid kit, and gave the man a shot for his pain. The morphine syrette was like a tiny tooth paste tube with a needle at the opening. The needle had a cap of thin glass which had to be broken before use.

When things settled down Bob reported looking around and seeing bandages hanging everywhere. A few days later, the flight surgeon saw Bob and told him they were going to give that bombardier two Purple Hearts. One for what the Germans did to him, and one for what Bob did to him. It seems the morphine is stored in a small tube with a thin glass covering. The glass is to be broken before it is administered. Bob in the excitement of the action, stabbed the poor guy without first breaking the glass, and the doctors had to pick many bits of glass out of the wound.

Bob really had a baptism of fire on his first mission.

The rest of our crew was to receive ours a day later!

The 390th Writes History

Mission History

570th Bomb Squadron, the 390th Bomb Group, 8th Air Force, received two Presidential Unit Citations, and it established a record for the most enemy aircraft destroyed by any one group on a single mission—62 German fighter aircraft.

Mission	Date	Target	Plane	Model
1	4/19/1944	Werl, Germany	*Sequatchee*	B-17, F-model
2	4/20/1944	La Glacerie, France	*Sequatchee*	B-17, F-model
3	4/22/1944	Hamm, Germany	*Sequatchee*	B-17, F-model
4	4/27/1944	La Glacerie, France	*Sequatchee*	B-17, F-model
5	4/28/1944	Sottevast, France	*Twenty-one or Bust*	B-17, G-model
6	4/29/1944	Berlin, Germany	*Twenty-one or Bust*	B-17, G-model
7	5/1/1944	Sarreguimines, France	*Twenty-one or Bust*	B-17, G-model
8	5/7/1944	Berlin, Germany	*Twenty-one or Bust*	B-17, G-model
9	5/8/1944	Berlin, Germany	*Twenty-one or Bust*	B-17, G-model
10	5/19/1944	Berlin, Germany	*Bomboogie*	B-17
11	5/20/1944	Brussels, Belgium	*Bomboogie*	B-17
12	5/23/1944	Melun, France	*Bomboogie*	B-17
13	5/25/1944	St. Valery, France	*Bomboogie*	B-17
14	5/27/1944	Strasbourg, France	*Bomboogie*	B-17
15	5/28/1944	Magdeburg, Germany	*Bomboogie*	B-17
16	5/29/1944	Leipzig, Germany	*Bomboogie*	B-17
17	6/4/1944	Boulogne, France	*Bomboogie*	B-17
18	6/5/1944	Abbeville, France	*Bomboogie*	B-17

Mission	Date	Target	Plane	Model
19	6/6/1944	Falaise, France	*Bomboogie*	B-17
20	6/7/1944	Nantes, France	*Bomboogie*	B-17
21	6/11/1944	Dinard-Pleurtvit, France	*Bomboogie*	B-17
22	6/15/1944	Misburg, Germany	*Bomboogie*	B-17
23	6/18/1944	Brunbuttel, Germany	*Bomboogie*	B-17
24	6/21/1944	Basdorf, Germany	*Bomboogie*	B-17
25	6/22/1944	Paris-St. Ouen, France	*Bomboogie*	B-17
26	6/25/1944	Area 5, France	*Bomboogie*	B-17
27	6/29/1944	Bohlen, Germany	*Bomboogie*	B-17
28	7/11/1944	Munich, Germany	*Bomboogie*	B-17
29	7/13/1944	Munich, Germany	*Bomboogie*	B-17
30	7/19/1944	Schweinfurt, Germany	*Bomboogie*	B-17
31	7/24/1944	Villedeau-les-Poeles	*Sweetheart of the Pas de Calaias*	B-17, G-model
32	7/25/1944	St. Lo, France	*Sweetheart of the Pas de Calaias*	B-17, G-model
33	7/31/1944	Munich, Germany	*Sweetheart of the Pas de Calaias*	B-17, G-model
34	8/4/1944	Harburg, Germany	*Sweetheart of the Pas de Calaias*	B-17, G-model
35	8/8/1944	St. Sylvan, France	*Sweetheart of the Pas de Calaias*	B-17, G-model

CHAPTER 10

The Combat Missions

MISSION 1
Werl, Germany
19 April 1944

We Finally Got our Call at 2:00 am

We dressed without any conversation and were trucked to the mess hall. I ate a few bites, went outside and walked to the briefing room. Our target was Werl, Germany, the Luftwaffe Airfield on the north end of the Ruhr Valley, in a very important industrial area.

I picked up my parachute, and rode a truck out to the flight line. The plane we were assigned for the mission was a war-weary B-17 (F model) named *Sequatchee*. A big Indian head was painted on the nose. It was an original bomb group plane and I thought it would be better in the junkyard or perhaps a museum. The position was "Tail End Charlie," where all rookie crews got their start. The standard practice was to put the newest crews in the oldest planes, flying in the most dangerous part of the formation.

The bomb run went smoothly, and when the lead plane dropped its bombs, I hit the toggle switch, unleashing my ten 500-pound bombs. The explosives covered the hangers, barracks, runways, and other buildings. All was routine, until I tried to close the bomb bay doors. I could not get them to come up. At first I thought it was a malfunction, but after we descended to a warmer altitude, they closed with no problem. This led me to believe that one of the gunners needing bladder relief went into the bomb bay and had watered down the closing mechanism. As the ice melted, everything worked and the doors came up. Never again did we experience this problem.

We encountered no enemy fighter planes, and the flak didn't seem too heavy. The flak

Sequatchee being flown on a bombing mission over France by a different crew. This shows a poor formation because only the one plane was dropping bombs. He was bombing either too soon or too late. When we flew Sequatchee we used her on our first four missions.

today didn't scare me but was rather fascinating, although later missions changed my thinking. The main thing I remember about this mission was how physically uncomfortable I had been. We were issued two-piece sets of 100% wool underwear. I had put mine on as the first layer, and spent most of my time on this mission scratching my butt. I never wore the bottom half again, and always wore a cotton T-shirt under the top half.

So, our first mission was logged; it was uneventful, and didn't seem like a very big deal.

Some Random Thoughts

Following are some things I learned quickly on the next few missions.

I was surprised and disappointed when we first arrived at the 390th base to learn most of the planes did not carry Bombsights. Formation flying seemed to preclude tight formation in which the bombardier kept his eye glued to the Bombsight, steering the plane through the Automatic Pilot, and this would certainly cause a collision. Within 30 seconds after the bombs hit, all one could see down there was smoke and dust. If the planes had to line up and go over one by one, it would take too long to get the entire Group over the target, and would give the flak gunners on the ground too much time to pick B-17s out of the air. The problem was solved with bombing by squadrons, groups, or even by wings. The lead plane did the aiming, and the first bomb was a smoke bomb. When the bombardiers following, saw it, they immediately dropped their bombs. We often bombed large cities on undercast (cloudy days), with a radar-equipped plane in the lead. We could not see the ground, and they could not see us, but each would know the other was there.

MISSION REGENSBURG

Bombardier and navigator in crowded nose

When the smoke bomb fell, we would drop with it, and more than rain fell out of the clouds. Any bomb that fell within the city limits was considered good bombing.

So much for precision bombing, but it was not all one-sided. The German radar had us on their scopes, and we lost many a plane to their flak gunners who never laid eyes on us.

In the air I was a bombardier for 15 or 20 minutes, but I was also the full time nose gunner. I never met a bombardier who had been to gunnery school, but there I was manning the most important gun position on the plane.

One of my duties was to be in constant communication with the rest of the crew via oxygen checks. The pilot flying the plane was on the radio command channel, which relayed information from the group or wing leader and the other nine of us were on intercom. I would call "oxygen check," every five or ten minutes, and from back to nose, I would hear, "Tail OK, waist OK, waist OK, ball turret OK, radio OK, top turret OK, pilots OK, navigator OK." On a couple of missions, I could tell that something was amiss, and that man would be attended to immediately. Usually a hose had become disconnected, and anoxia had set in. Anoxia is akin to intoxication, the speech is slurred and there is a feeling of euphoria, the person passes out and could eventually die.

I believe we were an unusually quiet crew, with little idle conversation. However, when German fighter planes were involved, the intercom came alive, reporting enemy action and numbers, and if we were being attacked, etc. Once we were back over the North Sea, the intercom again came to life. And only Andy could come up out of the ball, while the rest of us stayed at our stations in case of an emergency.

MISSION 2

La Glacerie, France
20 April 1944

A day after the Werl mission, we were in the air again, slated for a trip to La Glacerie, France, south of Cherbourg. We slept late that morning preparing for an afternoon departure. The target was a large concrete installation under construction, to be used as a launching pad for unmanned planes and rockets aimed at London. As of the day of the mission, construction was reported to be 90% complete.

Old Sequatchiee was again our plane, but we moved forward a notch in the formation. We carried ten 500-pound bombs in the bomb bay and one 1,000-pounder under each wing. We had a reduced fuel load because it was to be a short trip, and I will never know how Gillie and Baker got that old wreck of a plane off the ground with that weight of bombs. (The total weight of the load had been balanced between the fuel and the bombs and could not exceed 74,000 pounds.)

Our route took us past London, leaving the coast at Portsmouth, and turning onto the bomb run at the Channel Islands of Jersey and Guernsey. The flak was not heavy but we never encountered any more accurate. As we neared the target, flak burst right in front of

Sequatchee, an F-model B-17. An Indian chief was the painted nose art. She flew our crew on Missions 1, 2, 3 and 4.

us, and then another, and then another, and we immediately flew right through the smoke. I would say there were two dozen bursts, and if that gunner had fired any of those a fraction of a second later, we would have been a direct hit. The German 88-mm flak cannon was reputed to be the best gun of any type in any army, and I believe their gunners were world class. I was more scared on this mission than on any other I flew. I clamped my teeth down on my tongue so hard I could barely eat for a few days.

One plane in our Group suffered a direct hit and exploded, killing all crew members including my good buddy, McKinnon Cameron from Victorville, Salt Lake City, and Ardmore, who was the bombardier on that plane.

21 April 1944

We were awakened early for a mission, and after two hours in the air it was scrubbed (canceled) due to poor weather over the target. Weather reconnaissance or Mosquito planes would fly over the target a few hours before the bombers were due. They would radio weather condition reports back to the base that this day did not qualify for a mission.

Some Random Thoughts

On my first two missions, I quickly discovered the bomb run to be the most nerve-wracking time of the entire mission for me. Upon reaching the IP (Initial Point), the pilot had to refrain from any evasive action, fly straight and level in his formation. Flak and German fighter planes had to be ignored. The bomb run could take as long as 20 minutes. As the bomb bay doors slowly began to open, the tension increased, and I could sense silent pleading messages from the crew "Drop the bombs, please drop the bombs, damn it, drop the bombs." When the last bomb dropped and the doors began to close the Group would make a diving left turn to get out of flak. Every one gave a sigh of relief for the worst was behind us and we were on the way back to our base.

MISSION 3

Hamm, Germany
22 April 1944

Today we left the ground at 3:00 in the afternoon, headed for the Ruhr Valley again, to bomb the Marshalling Yards in the city of Hamm. This was known to be the busiest railroad yard in Europe. The entire Eighth Air Force was to take part in this mission. It was hard to imagine 1,000 planes bombing one city. We carried a normal load of ten 500-pound bombs, and had a good slot in the formation for the day in the high squadron.

We were on the return leg near Koblenz, when we were attacked by a number of Messerschmitt 109s who shot down one of our B-17s. Our Group was credited with getting six German aircraft. I did a lot of shooting, but couldn't say I hit anything. This was my first occasion to fire the guns from the nose position.

Now, we had flown three missions in four days, and we still had our hides intact.

23 April 1944

We were awakened for a 4:00 a.m. briefing, but while we were still on the ground, flares from the control tower signaled the mission had been scrubbed. Hooray! This would have been a tough one.

We quickly requested a two-day pass, which was approved in the middle of the afternoon. We cleaned up, donned dress uniforms and with warnings from our bunk mates, concerning the "Piccadilly Commandos." To quote Chuck Baker "These

One of London's double-decker busses

are ladies who earn top dollar." The ten of us boarded the train for our first trip to London. It was a nice two-hour ride with stops at Ipswich, Chelmsford, Colchester, and finally arriving at the Liverpool Street Station. We officers took one of the quaint taxis to the Jules Club on Jermyn Street in the heart of London, where officers could obtain rooms and meals for economy prices since it was operated by the American Red Cross. (Our enlisted men went in another direction, and I do not remember hearing anything about their fun and games.) A plaque at the Jules Club said it was the former home of Sir Isaac Newton who discovered gravity, and they recommended the Officer Mess at the Grovener House, the location of the Supreme Headquarters of the Allied Expedition Force (SHAEF), where General Eisenhower was in command. We walked to it and found a building covering a city block. I guess it would be comparable to the NYC Waldorf-Astoria. We walked around but could not find a mess for American officers. We did spot a small dining room where some men in uniform were dining, so we went in and sat down at a corner table. A string quartet was playing; there were linen napkins and table cloths, and lovely flower arrangements. I also noticed the other diners were high-ranking British officers with elegant women companions. The head waiter in formal attire came and handed each of us a menu, written entirely in French. I noted no prices, and then I knew for sure we were not in the American Officers' Mess. Munroe said, "I took French in my Kansas high school, and I'll read it to you," but after a minute or so he admitted he could not recognize one menu item. According to British wartime regulations, a restaurant could serve only a three course meal: soup, entree, and dessert, and could not charge over five shillings (about one US dollar). I picked up my menu, showed it to the waiter, and pointed to one thing in each section, and sat back wondering what I had ordered. When the food arrived, I saw I had ordered split pea soup, lobster, and a cherry tart. The soup was OK, the tart was probably made without sugar, and with one cherry. The lobster was the most delicious thing I had ever eaten. It had been steamed, taken apart, with the removed meat mixed with a light cheese sauce and reassembled. I cannot remember what the others ordered but when the check arrived; we each had been charged five shillings for the meal, five shillings for the table linens, five shillings for the music, and five shillings for the flowers, plus one or two other charges. It totaled over four pounds, or close to $20.00. We paid up, laughed, admitted we enjoyed it, and said it had been a memorable experience.

It had been a long day since 2:00 a.m. so we walked back to the club, and really enjoyed a good night of sleep. Oddly enough, we never again went back to that restaurant. The next morning we had pancakes and imitation sausage (by law sausage could only contain 5% meat).

After breakfast we headed out to the PX to replenish our toilet articles and other personal supplies. General Eisenhower had been wearing a custom designed garment everyone called an "Ike" jacket. They were very popular and we decided we should have one too. We each bought the fabric and some buttons at the PX, and took this to a tailor who would supply the lining. He measured us and said the garments would be ready the next time we came to town.

Fronts of British Coins, left to right, Row 1: Half Crown, Crown, Florin; Row 2: English Shilling, Scottish Shilling; Row 3: Half Penny, Threepence, Farthing, Sixpence & Penny. Backs of coins shown below.

We hadn't been off an air base since we left Nebraska some seven weeks before, and now we were ready to spend some money. The problem was the money itself. We were paid in British money, and the system wasn't easy to learn. There were twelve pennies in a shilling, and twenty shillings in a pound. There were five-pound notes worth about $20, pound notes worth $4, and ten shilling notes worth $2. There were the coins: crowns, half crowns, shillings, florins, thruppence, thrupenny bits, tuppence, penny, half pennies, and farthings. To make things worse, each one had a nickname. We had to learn what a "bob," "quid," "guinea," etc., was. Another problem was that every

> *There were twelve pennies in a shilling, and twenty shillings in a pound. There were five-pound notes worth about $20, pound notes worth $4, and ten shilling notes worth $2. There were the coins: crowns, half crowns, shillings, florins, thruppence, thrupenny bits, tuppence, penny, half pennies, and farthings.*
> *To make things worse, each one had a nickname.*

thing was scarce or severely rationed, and anything I wanted to buy was too expensive. Eateries had limited menus, and the food was unappetizing. Usually the best thing available would be seafood dishes.

By evening, we had purchased theater tickets to a production titled "Jill Darling." I had never been to a real Broadway type show, and I really enjoyed this entertainment.

After another night of sound sleep, the Red Cross lined up a tour of the city for us. I think the taxi was a Rolls Royce with a guide who showed us the places we had heard of and read about since we were kids. We saw Trafalgar Square, St. Paul's Cathedral, Big Ben, Westminster Abbey, the Tower of London, and Buckingham Palace. The guide even showed us some bombed out areas. The guy was quite witty and a real historian. I was disappointed when I asked to see Sherlock Holmes place on Baker Street, and he said it did not exist!

Later in the afternoon, we were back on the train, returning to Station 153. It is odd to say, but I was glad to get into my bed in the barracks, and I even felt like I was at home.

MISSION 4
La Glacerie, France
27 April 1944

2:00 am

Again we were rousted out of bed to fly. It was a repeat of Mission Two. The Group's bombing was off the mark on April 20, so we headed back to La Glacerie for another try. It took three to four hours to get the formation together and up to altitude, a boring time for all the crew except the pilots. After we got off the ground, I went into the bomb bay and pulled the cotter pins from the fuses in the bombs, two per bomb. I then went into the waist (the middle section of the plane), and laid down, wearing my parachute, and took a nap. I told the gunners if anything happens, put the ripcord in my hand and roll me out. However, if all is well, wake me when it is time to put on the oxygen mask.

There was plenty of flak today, but not as accurate as the last time and not a single plane

Each one of these dark spots is an exploding cannon shell (flak).

was shot down. I watched the bombs go down and signaled "Sur Le Nez" which meant "On the Nose" in French which had become the 390th motto.

When we landed, we counted many flak holes in *Sequatchee* but nothing vital had been struck.

Some Random Thoughts

On the first half dozen or so missions, I was able to sleep a bit en route to the destination. After that, I had seen so many things that happened to other planes that I could not relax, so I stayed in the nose. On one of the early missions, we were over enemy territory and either we or the plane ahead of us, or above us, was out of position. Their ball turret gunner started firing over us and one of the brass cartridges from his .50-caliber machine gun came flying through the plexiglas in front of me, caromed off my steel helmet, and hit Bob Munroe in his chest knocking him down. We had flak vests on and neither of us suffered injury.

After each mission, as we left the plane, we were met by a flight surgeon. He offered each of us an ounce of medicinal alcohol to calm our nerves before we went into debriefing. The drink was Scotch whiskey, which was something I had no experience with. After my first mission, I sniffed it, tested it with my tongue, and then unobtrusively poured it on the ground. After the second mission, I poured it in the coffee a Red Cross lady handed me, tasted it, and poured it on the ground. The third time, I put it in a cup of cocoa, tasted it, and poured it on the ground. The fourth time, I mixed it with canned milk, tasted it, and arrived at the conclusion I would never become a Scotch drinker. Our tail gunner had been watching me and said what I was doing was criminal. In addition, he recommended I give my ration to him. This I did. After several ounces on an empty stomach, the stories he told the debriefing officer were fantastic. After he left our crew, I always offered the tail gunner my ration and was never turned down.

MISSION 5

Sottevast, France
28 April 1944

Today we were awakened very early as usual, and were scheduled for a mission to another rocket launching installation at Sottevast, near Cherbourg, France.

I had a big surprise and shock when we arrived at the hardstand. There, instead of *Sequatchee*, was a G-model B-17 with a Black Jack hand (Ace and Jack of Spades) painted on the nose and painted above were the words, "Twenty-one or Bust." The shock was that I had never been in a B-17 with a chin turret and had never fired from a turret. The chin turret window with .50-caliber machine guns was a big improvement over the F model B-17 with one hand-held gun.

Fortunately, Wittleder, our waist gunner, came to my rescue by saying he could "check me out" in this new contraption. The sun had not come up yet, so we had to work in the dark. In *Sequatchee* there had been one machine gun sticking out the plexiglas nose and to charge it (get a round into the chamber) all I had to do was pull back a handle on the side of the gun, all the way back and let it go. This forced the bullet into firing mode. The control resembled bicycle handlebars and was off to the right side. When they were to be used, one just pivoted it over to the center of the nose. The charging button and triggers were right at hand. An optical gun sight was suspended from the top of the nose.

The new model turned out to be very different. Wittleder told me to go up to my seat and he would stand under the turret. We would check to see that all was working. He yelled up for me to charge it and then pull the trigger, while he looked up into the left gun. I did this. He said both were working and that I should repeat my action and he would check the right gun. So I charged it again, pulled the trigger and B-RRRRRRPPP went across the field and dark sky. In an arc went .50-caliber bullets and more noticeably, tracer bullets. The guns

Twenty-one or Bust

He said both were working and that I should repeat my action and he would check the right gun. So I charged it again, pulled the trigger and B-RRRRRRPPP went across the field and dark sky. In an arc went .50-caliber bullets and more noticeably, tracer bullets. The guns and ammo had been installed before we arrived and I had not noted that they gravity fed into the chamber. I was horrified at what I had done, and Wittleder said he thought his head had been blown off.

and ammo had been installed before we arrived and I had not noted that they gravity fed into the chamber. I was horrified at what I had done, and Wittleder said he thought his head had been blown off. The nose guns were always loaded with armor-piercing, incendiary bullets, and with every fifth one, a tracer bullet. On the ground, the guns were always pointed up to their maximum elevation (about 30 degrees) and as they passed over our base, they put on a very good show.

On with the mission—our target in France was hidden in an odd shaped piece of woods and we flew all over northern France, trying to find it, being shot at all the while. Bombing rules in France and the Low Countries were very strict. We were not to drop unless we were sure of the target and we had no idea about this one, so we flew back across the Channel and laid the bombs in the water.

I had been concerned during the whole flight to France as to where the bullets had landed this morning. The .50-caliber gun is a mean weapon capable of much damage. It has a range of about four miles. When we landed, the crew chief told me Colonel Gemmell wanted to see me, and this increased my apprehension so I hotfooted it to the orderly room. He began by asking me why I fired my guns this morning. I did not want to give him a song and a dance, so I just said "No excuse, Sir." He opened a thick book, and showed me a dozen or more pages and asked me if I would like to read all the things he could do to me. He added, this would cause both of us many problems. He suggested I should make a contribution of ten pounds to the Red Cross. That was almost $40.00 in American money. I hated to part with that money but it closed the situation. I was very glad to get it behind me. My firing of a gun while on the ground was not an isolated incident. I knew of a navigator who fired one of the side nose guns into the ground, right in front of the plane. I also heard of a ball turret gunner who fired both his guns one morning. They were about two feet above the ground and cut a Jeep in half.

This crew had Twenty-one or Bust before we had it, but I do not know who they were.

By now, I had flown enough missions to realize I had the best position on the plane. The pilots, in addition to the mental stress, were subjected to strenuous physical exertion. Formation flying was just plain hard work. Munroe, the navigator, was just behind me in the nose. He could not see much because two machine guns and I were blocking the view. He was nervous and rarely sat down. He was usually pacing back and forth as we flew toward the target, and continued pacing for half of the way home. When the flak got really heavy, he would back up to me, and in addition, scrunch against my back. I think he figured any thing coming in the nose would have to go through me before it got to him. It irked me and I told him if the Germans did not kill him, I would. He said he was just protecting me from anything coming in through the rear.

The top turret gunner had to stand all the time. In addition, the waist gunners stood a lot but had some wooden ammo boxes to sit on when there was no action. They were in the cold and windy part of the plane. The ball turret gunner was really cramped in that ball and could scarcely move. The tail gunner was also cramped but could not stand. He had a lot of breeze coming in around the tail wheel. The radio operator had a seat in his little room and I don't know how he spent his time. I don't think he ever fired his gun. In my position, I could see all that happened in front of the plane and all that plexiglas surrounding me gave me a 180-degree view up, down, and on both sides. I liked the position because I could see everything and I hated it because I could see everything. I HAD A FRONT ROW SEAT AT

The bombardier is concerned primarily with those gun turrets he is most likely to operate. He is almost always responsible for control of the nose turrets in heavy and very heavy aircraft.
BENDIX CHIN TURRET (B-17)
The chin turret of the B-17 operates electrically by remote control from the bombardier's seat directly above it. It moves 86° to either side in azimuth, 26° above and 46° below horizontal in elevation. It uses the N-8 or N-6A optical gunsight. The bombardier's seat remains stationary; as he turns the gunsight, the guns swing around beneath. The bombardier's control unit, housing the gun-sight, pivots out from its stowed position on his right and locks in place in front of him.

THE WAR.

MISSION 6

Berlin, Germany

29 April 1944

For the third day in a row, we were awakened to fly at 2:00 am. The briefing officer walked across the room, pulling the curtain, and when I saw the ribbon went all way to "Big B," Berlin, I thought, "Horrors, the most dreaded target in Germany."

We were assigned to fly close to the front of the bomber stream. Next day the newspapers said there were 1,000 bombers over this target. It was so overcast we could not see the ground.

We were following a Pathfinder, (a radar equipped plane). And when he dropped his smoke bomb, we dumped ours. The flak was extremely heavy and persistent and we were in it a very long time. The aiming point was the Fredric Strasse (Fredrick Street Station). I was hoping we were within the city limits.

I do not know where my head was when a huge piece of flak came through the plexiglas in front of me, and went out through the top of the plane's nose, hitting the windshield right in front of co-pilot Baker. The cockpit's thick glass, although shattered, remained intact and

In my position, I could see all that happened in front of the plane and all that plexiglas surrounding me gave me a 180-degree view up, down, and on both sides. I liked the position because I could see everything and I hated it because I could see everything.
I HAD A FRONT ROW SEAT AT THE WAR.

Suddenly we were in heavy flak, and one burst right under us. There was this loud explosion, the plane bucked, and started to roll over. I thought we had hit a brick wall and were going down. In a flash, I threw my feet back over my head, pulling all my connections off the wall. I stomped past Munroe, opened the escape hatch, wrapped my arms around my shins, and started to roll out. He grabbed me and kept me from jumping. He saw what had happened and I had not. Fletcher's Castoria had been hit, and was about to ram us.

kept the piece from coming through. I thought to myself, "It is not fair. The pilots have three inches of bulletproof glass in front of them and I have only a ¼ inch of plexiglas."

I dropped the bombs and a few minutes later there was a heavy burst, near the right wing. It hit the number three engine and the pilots had to quickly shut it down and feather the propeller. The remaining three engines were not pulling full power, so we began lagging behind. Shortly we were all alone over Germany. It was not a happy situation. Baker writes in his diary, "Art started singing 'Coming in on a wing and a prayer'." I cannot believe I was that numb.

Before long, we were joined by a couple of straggler planes and soon we were leading the bunch of cripples back to England. I noticed a plane flying on the left slightly above and behind us. The name painted on the nose was "Fletcher's Castoria." The undercast below us was solid, so there were no landmarks and none of us knew where we were. Suddenly we were in heavy flak, and one burst right under us. There was this loud explosion, the plane bucked, and started to roll over. I thought we had hit a brick wall and were going down. In a flash, I threw my feet back over my head, pulling all my connections off the wall. I stomped past Munroe, opened the escape hatch, wrapped my arms around my shins, and started to roll out. He grabbed me and kept me from jumping. He saw what had happened and I had not. Fletcher's Castoria had been hit, and was about to ram us. Our pilots had just about turned us upside down to keep from being hit. (I had often wondered how I would react if our plane was going down, but I found that I would jump without hesitation.)

Later, I asked Bob where we were when this excitement occurred and he said he was not sure but we might have been over Aachen, on the border of Holland and Germany. We were the last plane in our Group to make it back that day. And what a day it had been. We had been over the worst target in Germany; we had been in the air over ten hours and landed

Nose Art
Examples of the "Nose Art" with which we decorated our planes

Betty Boop, "Pistol Packin' Mama"

Cash & Carrie

Virgin Sturgeon

Behind the 8-ball

Bullet hole just missed her.

almost out of fuel. We returned an hour later than any other plane. The Group lost one B-17 that day and came very close to also losing us!

Note: To my younger readers, Fletcher's Castoria was a famous laxative for children. Several years ago, I read an obituary in the Eighth Air Force Historical Society magazine that the pilot of that plane had been a Lt. Bill Fletcher. Following the crash he was a POW (Prisoner of War) in Germany for over a year.

MISSION 7

Sarreguimines, Germany
01 May 1944

May Day, we were summoned at 12:30 a.m. and at 4:30 a.m. we were airborne. We practiced formation flying until about 8:30 a.m. and then were briefed to bomb a target in northern France. We developed engine trouble and had to return to base. Upon landing, we were sent immediately to a briefing to Sarreguimines, south of Saarbrucken, Germany. As the wheels left the ground, the plexiglass cover of the top turret flew off and lodged in the leading edge of the horizontal stabilizer. We landed and were hustled to another plane and told to catch up with the Group. All went smoothly. We clobbered the target and headed home.

Suddenly we were attacked from the rear by a bunch of German ME-109s and Coburn in the tail had his hands full. He said the whole German Air Force was shooting at him and to make things worse a large piece of flak came through the tail, cutting a big gash in the wall beside him, and hit his ammo chute, bumping his foot aside. Suddenly, a bunch of our P-51s arrived, dropped their belly tanks, and lit into the Germans. What a welcome sight. It was almost dark when we landed. It had been a long day but we had seven missions to our credit. Our Group was credited with downing three German planes and losing none. Coburn was pretty well shaken as we went into debriefing. A day or two later, Coburn told Gilmore he was leaving the crew and nothing would ever induce him to get into another airplane.

This action brought up some interesting Army Air Corps policies. Every flyer was a volunteer. No one was ever drafted to fly, (except our Jimmy Stewart). I believe the US Army Air Corps was the only unit of the military in World War II, in which a man could refuse to take part in combat. In all other branches of service one could be court-marshaled, or even given the firing squad. I, for one, approved of this policy. I wouldn't want to fly with a man who wouldn't or couldn't perform his duties because of fear. It would badly impair the efficiency of that crew and could lead to disaster. All of us were nervous about the excursions over the continent and at times just plain scared to death. We hung in there and kept on flying. We hated to see Tom leave the crew but not one of us tried to change his mind.

Tom's decision resulted in his being busted from sergeant down to private, with corresponding loss of pay, and he also lost flying pay. He was assigned to a bomb loading crew, which was very hard work and usually done at night. I suppose there were defections from other crews but he was the only one I knew of. Personally, I would have been more scared of telling my crew I was leaving, than I was of flying over Berlin.

The very next night, Wittleder got sick while in the latrine and was diagnosed as having a heart attack. He was taken off the crew and replaced by Raymond Jankowski, who flew with us on the remainder of our missions. He was from Detroit, Michigan, and a quiet fellow who fit into the crew very quickly. We had no permanent replacement for Coburn, but a succession of tail gunners. Several were with us on only one mission.

MISSION 8

Berlin, Germany

07 May 1944

We celebrated this day by going back to Berlin. We were to lead the Low Squadron to the same city over the same route, aiming at the same target, and getting shot at by the same guns. We sure were giving those gunners down there plenty of target practice. It was a Pathfinder (radar) mission with 100% clouds covering the city.

It was an unusually cold day and when I tried to open the bomb bay doors, they were frozen shut. To open the doors, a mechanical rod had to be in the correct position. While trying to free this rod, it went into SALVO position in which the doors flew open and all ten bombs dropped at once. At the time I should have dropped the bombs, Gilmore was flying the plane, and overshot the Lead Squadron. For a few minutes, we and the five planes following us were out over Berlin all by ourselves. Both Gillie and I received comments from the crew about our performances. They said all I had done that day was the spring plowing for a German farmer, and Gilmore was trying to form his own Air Force. We saw no German fighter planes and lost none of our bombers. For a target like Berlin, this was a relatively uneventful day.

Some Random Thoughts

FLEIGERABWEHRKANONEN was the German word for what they were shooting at us. Back in the States, we called it anti-aircraft fire. The British called it Ack Ack. I do not know what they called it in the Pacific, but the printable word we used was Flak, and it was nasty stuff. At first those puffs of black smoke seemed harmless enough, but after a while we found out what it could do to us. With each mission, we became more nervous about being over Berlin. We encountered 105-mm shells and on several occasions we were subjected to exploding rockets. All these were designed to explode at our altitude or upon contact. Flak did not make a nice round hole like a bullet but rather detonated into jagged fragments, which tore ugly holes upon contact. The Germans had two systems of firing; they could track us and shoot at us as we went along. Depending on where we were, it might last for a few minutes or almost an hour. The other system was a "box barrage" and here radar would calculate our path and altitude, the guns would wait for a signal, and all would fire at once into that box. We might be flying along without any flak and suddenly the sky in front would turn black with smoke. Another group flying ahead of us might see two or three planes go down and in a minute you would be in it too. Sitting there in the nose, between 4,800-horsepower engines, I did not often hear any of it but when I did, I knew they were too darn close. I have had fliers tell me they saw shells come up near their plane to the top of their trajectory and fall back down without exploding.

Years after the war, I read stories of slave labor in munitions factories, risking their lives to sabotage the products being produced, and recalled this about the flak. We might be flying in sub zero temperatures and I would be sitting there shivering from the cold, but at the first burst of flak, I would turn off my heated suit, unzip my jacket, loosen my scarf, and wipe the sweat from my brow.

MISSION 9

Berlin, Germany
08 May 1944

Back to Berlin once more. This is getting monotonous. It was almost a carbon copy of the mission yesterday except I got my bombs off on schedule. Gilmore repeated his performance of overshooting the Lead Squadron again. One sad exception, we lost three B-17s in the extremely heavy flak. We landed with less than 100 gallons of fuel (about 20 minutes of flying time), only seven quarts of oil, and one burned-out engine. All in all, a very BAD DAY.

10 May 1944

We were up again at 2:00 a.m. but after flying five hours, the mission was scrubbed (canceled) due to weather conditions. There would be "No Mission Credit." Therefore, we came back to our barracks, ready to hit the sack, and then were told we had a two-day pass if we wanted it, and we could catch the train in 15 minutes. Unbelievably, we made that train headed for London. We intended to stay in the Regent Palace Hotel in Piccadilly, but when we arrived we found it had been hit by a "buzz bomb" earlier in the day. The top two floors were not available (these floors were usually reserved for American personnel). We found other lodging nearby. Baker and I decided to do some sightseeing but we soon realized we were exhausted and retired for the night. Next morning we visited the tailor shop on Jermyn Street to pick up our new Eisenhower jackets. They were very nice with one exception—the tailor had lined them in a brilliant red satin which meant we had to wear them buttoned all the time. "Could not look unmilitary, you know." In the afternoon, we visited the famous Madam Taussaud's Wax Museum. Later after dinner, Munroe and I enjoyed "The Love Racket" at the theater. After dark, we roamed Piccadilly Circus with our five gunners.

Back at the base the next day, we were greeted with very sad news. Lt. Corcorean and crew were flying the plane (Twenty-One or Bust), and flying in our position, had been shot down. We had flown that plane on its 21st mission and they took it on its 22nd, (actually, it only flew twenty-one and a half missions). It could have been named Twenty-one and Bust. After the war, I learned that Corky and his co-pilot had been killed and the other eight men who had bailed out had been captured and were prisoners of war. I always have believed the two pilots had stayed with the plane until the others were out and then were not able to save themselves.

Some Random Observations Related to a Mission

There was no such thing as a typical mission which is usually described as "hours of complete boredom, and minutes of absolute terror." I noticed a war movie always had to have a crummy love story to make it watchable. A real mission generally went something like this. The mission would be announced between 7:00 and 9:00 p.m. the prior evening by hoisting the blue flag over each squadron area, closing the bars in the service clubs, and word of mouth. Therefore, if a mission was scheduled, everyone knew it at once. I would go back to the barracks, write a quick V-Mail letter home, get my cleanest clothes ready, get into bed, and lapse into neverland mode. This was called "nervous in the service." Sleep was difficult with nineteen other bodies twisting and turning. I am sure all of them (except maybe Chuck Baker) were as tense as I was. It varied but usually around 2:00 am, an enlisted man came into the room and called the names of the crew commanders who would be flying. If Gilmore's name was not called, I would roll over, and be asleep in 30 seconds. If we were called, I popped up and began moving. I always gave my leather A-2 flying jacket and my pistol to someone to hold for me until I got back. I started dressing by putting on a pair of wool cushion-sole socks, the top half of my long johns over my cotton T-shirt, wool pants, shirt, wool sweater, coveralls, heavy flying jacket, and boots. We were trucked to the mess hall, where I looked over that unappetizing breakfast, said "Ugh," and did little more than nibble. We walked or were trucked to the briefing room, which usually had 200 or more men crowded in. Most of the men were puffing on cigarettes and because of the smoke, one could barely see across the room.

The center of attention was a large curtain covering the front wall. The briefing might be held by the group commander but more likely a squadron commander. It would start out with a few unimportant comments but quickly got into the important information: take-off time, weather reports, radio information, probability of fighter plane attacks, flak areas, etc. The anxiety level rose and finally the officer would go to the left side of the room, grab the curtain, and slowly pull it to the right, revealing a wall size map of Europe with England on the left and Russia on the right. A black ribbon starting at Framlingham zigzagged across the map to the target. If the ribbon was short, there were sighs of relief but if it was long, there were moans and groans.

At this point, the gunners left and were trucked to the plane and the pilots remained for more detailed information. The navigators and radio operators were trucked elsewhere to be briefed, as were the bombardiers. We were shown aerial photos of the target area with the route going in to the target. We were also given the bomb load and weather over the target. After the briefings and before we entered the plane, a chaplain would conduct a brief prayer service meeting. It was non-denominational and out of the 200 men flying that day, maybe two dozen attended. I always went representing our crew and hoping it would increase our odds of coming back. After the service, some clown would yell "let us spray" so we all lined up, opened our mouths, and the same chaplain gave us each a throat spray. The air at our flying altitudes was as dry as the Sahara Desert and we all had a cough known as the ETO (European Theatre Operation) hack.

Worship Services were held every Sunday morning and these were better attended, but not nearly as well attended as the Saturday night dances at the officers club, which were always attended by several truckloads of British girls from the area. One of the more attractive girls was a very energetic and athletic dancer. Baker was also a good dancer and they seemed to gravitate towards each other, making a dynamic duo. She always wore a short, pleated skirt. I never knew her name but all the officers in the 390th knew her as "Purple Panties."

We each had to pick up our own parachutes before we went to the plane and one of the co-pilot's duties was to pick up Escape Packs for each man. These packs would help a downed man needing to escape capture. They contained caffeine pills, high-energy pills, hard chocolate, razor, fishing line, hooks, compass, waterproof maps of the area, some used bills of French, Dutch, and Belgian money, and some other items. At the plane, our crew and the ground crew were chewing the fat and primping the plane for the journey. The gunnery crew had installed their guns and the ground crew installed mine. It required a scaffold, some tools, and a bit of expertise to get my guns into the chin turret. I would go into the bomb bay to check the bomb load, (usually ten 500-pound bombs). I also would check the bomb shackles, and examine the 20 fuses to make sure there was an arming wire in each one. All this done, I got into the nose and checked the bomb panel to see if there was a light on for each bomb showing its location on the racks. I made sure my throat mike, ear phones, oxygen mask, flak suit, leather helmet, steel helmet goggles, Mae West, and one-man life raft were accounted for. The intercom and finally the oxygen pressure was tested. I then peeled off my outer clothes, got into the heated suit, put a coverall on, then a heavy flying jacket, and made sure I had my mittens.

Should I have forgotten any of these items, I would have been in real trouble since I would be five miles above Mother Earth with air temperatures below zero and no heat on the plane. Ice would form on my jacket as my warm breath coming from the oxygen mask hit the cold air. My parachute weighed some twenty pounds, the Mae West a couple of pounds, the steel helmet another couple of pounds, the life raft another twenty pounds, and the flak suit about 30 pounds. If I had been weighed with all that on, I bet the scales would have registered at least 200 pounds. My scrawny body objected to that, so once I got it all in place I usually sat down and never left my seat until we were almost returning to England.

After we got over the water, I check-fired my guns. The hours it took to assemble the formation and climb to altitude were dull and boring but once we were underway I began to relax and I detached my mind from this situation. Not till the first burst of flak or sighting of enemy planes, did I come back to reality. On the bomb run, anything and everything could and did happen. I reacted to the best of my ability without thinking about it.

We always said that until we dropped the bombs, we were working for Uncle Sam, but once I said "bombs away," we were working for ourselves. Now our only target was to get these ten bodies safely back to England. We spent the next couple of days, breaking in new crews and in formation flying.

16 MAY 1944

Today word came that each member of our crew was awarded the Air Medal (routinely awarded to crews surviving five or six missions).

An Oak Leaf would follow for subsequent missions. There was no formal ceremony. Just a stop by the orderly room to pick it up along with a mimeographed citation authorized by General Curtis Lemay who later commanded the 20th Air Force. I wrapped my medal and mailed it home to my parents. Within a week, the Air Corps sent to both the Covington and Lexington, Virginia, newspapers an article that was printed.

Joyce, Bob, Doris, and Art in London park. The natives are friendly

MISSION 10

Berlin, Germany

19 May 1944

It had been nine days since we had flown a mission but today we were being called upon to fly. At the briefing when the captain pulled the curtain, I thought to myself, "Damn, Berlin again!" I believe the Eighth Air Force could not find Berlin without the 390th showing them the way. In the morning when we got to the flight line we found a different B-17 waiting. It had no decoration on the nose, just the word "BOMBOOGIE." It had flown many missions but for some strange reason, we all felt quite comfortable with our new chariot. This plane was a replacement for *Twenty-one or Bust*, the plane which we had flown on missions five through nine.

Today's mission parroted our previous trips to "Big B," a pathfinder mission, the same route in and out, same aiming point, same heavy flak, but there were differences. On the bomb run, we carried a new type bomb named "jellied gasoline." I was not happy having it

Today's mission parroted our previous trips to "Big B," a pathfinder mission, the same route in and out, same aiming point, same heavy flak, but there were differences. On the bomb run, we carried a new type bomb named "jellied gasoline." I was not happy having it aboard because it was unstable and would explode if hit by flak.

aboard because it was unstable and would explode if hit by flak. In later years, it was made safer, but got a bad reputation in the Vietnam War where it was called Napalm. A second difference in this mission was the rockets being fired at us. When we were leaving the target, according to Munroe's diary we endured nineteen minutes of fighter attacks, all directed at our squadron. Our whole crew was shooting in return. Fred, in the ball turret, sent a Focke-Wulf 190, the German's finest fighter plane, to its reward. The 390th plane on our left was hit in the wing tank and we watched as the ten crewmembers bailed out before it exploded. Again, this was not a fun day, but now the Log Book read Mission Ten Complete.

MISSION 11

Brussels, Belgium
20 May 1944

We were briefed for the railroad yards in Brussels, Belgium. The target was obscured by clouds so the mission leader ordered us to Antwerp, Holland where conditions were the same. Since we were running low on fuel, we dumped our bomb load in the North Sea and returned to the UK. It was a "milk run," but we received credit for Mission 11. By now we considered ourselves seasoned veterans. There is an old Army definition that "A seasoned veteran is one who had been assaulted and peppered by the enemy."

Some Random Thoughts

During the operational missions, I lost my appetite. When we were awakened so early, I always went to the mess hall, but when I sat down and looked at the food I would wonder why I had come. There was never a fresh egg, only powdered. The cereal I remember was a round British thing that looked and tasted like a piece of asbestos insulation. There was never real milk, only powdered which was reconstituted. I had visions of a sleepy GI dumping the white powder into a large vat of water and stirring it once. The result was big lumps of powder floating in bluish water. It did not do a thing to help the cereal. We did get canned orange and pineapple juices. The other meals tended to be stew, hash, or spaghetti. I guess

During the operational missions, I lost my appetite. When we were awakened so early, I always went to the mess hall, but when I sat down and looked at the food I would wonder why I had come. There was never a fresh egg, only powdered. The cereal I remember was a round British thing that looked and tasted like a piece of asbestos insulation.

it was good, but it all tasted the same to me.

Most of the meat served was mutton. As you approached the dining hall and heard a lot of bleating inside, you knew what was on the menu. Sugar and any condiments were scarce, and the only desserts I remember were raisin and dried apple pies. Very little of what we had to eat came from Britain, but came by ship in a box or a can from the USA.

I did not complain for I realized how much better off we were than the British people. There were three mess halls on the base in three separate buildings. One for ground officers, another for ground enlisted, and the third for combat crews, both officers and enlisted men. The only one I ever ate in was the Combat Crew Mess. It was shaped like the letter H with the officers on one side, the gunners on the other and the kitchen in between. When we were flying we always missed the noon meal and if we got back late, the gunners' side would be closed and they ate with us. The grapevine said the ground officers' mess was better than the combat mess and the ground enlisted mess was not as good. No surprise there. The last few months I was there, a new item was put on the menu and I was delighted. Some genius got this bright idea of mixing powdered eggs with powdered milk, and adding sugar and vanilla flavoring to make imitation eggnog. It was not cold, but I thought it tasted good and I guzzled all I could.

May 22, 1944
My 23rd Birthday

It was a non-flying day so I had lots of time to ponder my situation. I could not clearly remember any birthday since high school. I began to wonder how I became so old in such a short time. It had been a busy and exciting time. There had been many "firsts," unusual experiences. Today, I thought, I am a 23-year-old man faced with the thought that there were so many more things which I wished to accomplish, but also realized that tomorrow I could go on a mission and be killed. All in all, it was a most depressing day, and if I had liked Scotch whiskey, I would have quaffed a few!

MISSION 12

Melun, France
23 May 1944

We were awakened at 1:30 a.m. and airborne by 6:30 am. Our mission today was to bomb a German air base located at Melun, south of Paris. The weather conditions were the same as those on 20 May. After groping around, we finally returned to base with a full load of bombs. I do not know what our armament crew had to say when we returned with all those bombs, which they had to unload during the night, but I bet they were most unhappy. I knew the procedure to load them was to put a steel cable around each bomb, one at a time.

Using a hand operated winch, each bomb was lifted into the bomb bay. I just assumed they lowered and removed them in a reverse procedure. Forty or so years later at a 390th Bomb Group Reunion, I met one of our armament loaders and I asked him about my assumption. Smiling sheepishly, he said, "First we screwed the two fuses out of each bomb to immobilize them. Then we placed a borrowed bed mattress and springs (from our barracks) on the concrete pad under the bay of the plane. The last step was simple, we toggled (dropped) each bomb onto the ground, one by one!"

All this was happening in the dark of night while the "Brass" slept!

MISSION 13

St. Valerie, France

25 May 1944

Again we were up at 1:30 am. The Wing (the leading officer) was making us think we had a rough one coming. We were briefed to strike a gun emplacement about a half-mile inland from the English Channel in the town of St. Valerie. We took off and were in the air only 3 hours, 35 minutes. Missions do not get shorter than that, and I do not remember any flak. After all those trips to Berlin, we had received three easy ones, and we appreciated that. The 13th mission was not unlucky. We did not know at the time but all those trips to Northern France were to soften up the German Army in preparation for the Invasion of Normandy, France. Only eleven days later US troops arrived on the beach. About this time, our Commanding Officer, Colonel Edgar Witten, was promoted and moved up to the Thirteenth Wing. This meant he would be leaving the 390th. To date he had been the first and only Commanding Officer and was highly regarded as our leader. Colonel Frederick Ott, who had been in a desk job in London, came to replace him.

MISSION 14

Strasbourg, Germany

27 May 1944

Up at 1:45 a.m. and briefed to strike a synthetic oil plant at Strasbourg in southeast Germany. As we approached the continent near Dieppe, the group in front of us took an awesome dose of flak. One plane was hit and exploded, taking the planes on either side down also. It was a spectacular sight. I did not relish flying into flak like that, just after seeing thirty men killed. As we approached the target on the bomb run, we could see the Alps Mountains in the far distance and that was another spectacular sight. Flak over the target was moderate, but they did knock down one plane from our Group. Jaffe, a bombardier in another crew in our barracks was wounded in the arm by a piece of flak, which earned him an Oak Leaf Cluster on his previously awarded Purple Heart.

MISSION 15

Magdeburg, Germany

28 May 1944

Early in the morning, three of the operational crews in our barracks were tapped to fly a mission to bomb an oil refinery at Magdeburg, Germany, southwest of Berlin.

Not long after we reached the hardstand and *Bomboogie*, the mission was delayed for two hours. I suddenly developed a very odd feeling about this delay, so I borrowed a bicycle and pedaled back to my barracks. I had a couple of Hershey chocolate bars stashed away in my footlocker. Just in case I did not come back from this mission, I ate all of them.

About halfway across the North Sea, I heard some of the most heavenly music imaginable, and it was coming from inside my head. It sounded like a huge symphony orchestra combined with pipe organs. I began to wonder if I was dead or would soon be. Strangely, this did not seem to bother me. Our Group was leading the Eighth Air Force this day, and therefore we would be the first over the target. Our escort was hovering above us and suddenly they jettisoned their disposable fuel tanks and headed back to intercept a flight of German fighter planes. As we started on the bomb run I heard Baker say, "Something is wrong here, we are supposed to be the first group over the target, but there is another one out there!" It developed to be a formation of 40 or 50 German fighter planes. They came in a shallow dive (twelve o'clock high) and firing away. One Focke Wulf 190 picked me and I returned fire. My tracers passed on his right side and with a slight movement of my guns, my bullets were hitting his fuselage. I saw an explosion on his wing. He dove down to fly under us, and he blew up in a fireball right under us. I saw more fighters on the left and I continued firing until my ammo ran out. By that time, I realized every gun on Bomboogie was empty as well. We were flying at 200 mph and the Germans were flying over 400 mph. We were closing at 600 mph, and that doesn't give one time to plan a course of action. I know this whole episode took 20 seconds because that is all the firing time my guns had. The guns fire 600 rounds per minute and each gun had 200 rounds and at some point during this action, I dropped my bombs, which I have no recollection of doing. When I had time to look around at our formation, I noted that five of our planes were missing; fifty men were gone in twenty seconds! I do not know where our escort went, but they were of no use to us today. The worst part of the mission today was after landing and debriefing we had to return to the barracks. The sight of those twelve empty beds confronted us. Why were we the only crew that was blessed to return?

Matthias and crew were on their twenty-fourth mission, and Ingram and crew were on their seventh (Ingram had played violin, and the cows in the adjoining pasture would come and listen to the music when he played.) We saw no parachutes during the battle, and assumed that all had been killed. However, after the war, Matthias turned up at the 390th Reunion at Long Beach, California, and we learned that Matthias and crew had become POWs and the navigator lost his leg. All in Ingram's plane had been killed. Our Group was credited with shooting down seven German fighter planes, and they knocked down five of our bombers. They possibly lost seven men to our loss of fifty. A very bad exchange. The 390th Bomb Group had flown 113 missions and only once before had they lost more than five planes.

On the return flight from Magdeburg that day, I contemplated the music I had heard and decided my message meant "You will not be killed ; You will be safe; You need not be afraid." From then on, I flew 20 more missions with no concerns at all.

Another description of this same incident over Magdeburg is found in *Mission 376, Battle over the Reich: 28 May 1944* by Ivo de Jong:

> One of the other aircraft in the Lead Squadron of the 390th Bomb Group was B-17G 42-31974 Bomboogie, piloted by Lts. Robert C. Gilmore and Charles N. Baker. The latter recorded the events in his diary, after his safe return to Framlingham that evening: 'When we arose early this morning, little did we realize we would come home to an almost empty barracks. Both Matthias and Ingram went down, no chutes reported. Our target for today was Magdeburg. Got usual flak in, for our route was straight for Berlin, which was a feint. However, we turned south and to the target some 80 miles before Berlin.
>
> With our bomb bay doors open and just three minutes before bombs away, we noticed high at one o'clock, five P-51s drop their belly tanks, and head for six o'clock; evidently fighters had been sighted there. About one minute later Gillie nudged me and pointed out front at another formation. I picked up the binoculars and what I saw could chill a persons blood for instead of B-17s all I saw were two-engined and single-engined ships.
>
> Here they came, some forty or fifty of them heading straight for us and every one firing. 20-mm cannon shells were exploding all around us. With this one pass they knocked Ingram, who was flying on our right wing down, and also Matthias who was right above us.
>
> As these fellows came by, I got a picture of one. At this time Ordel [bombardier Arthur W. Ordel, author] was shooting at one at a hundred yards, which then exploded. Hope I got it in the picture. I hadn't noticed, but later Gillie told me an Fw 190 had to turn up in a ninety degree bank in order to come between us over our left wing. Don't know how many Jerries went down on this pass, but rest assured there were a good many.
>
> As they went by, they began to queue up at once to come through again. Made a pass from eleven and from one. Got usual flak on route out as we 'sweated', even shot at us as we were going out over the Channel.'
>
> —*Mission 376, Battle over the Reich: 28 May 1944* by Ivo de Jong, Hikoki Publications LTD 2003.

MISSION 16

Leipzig, Germany

29 May 1944

After two VERY rough missions, I thought we would be given a break. Instead, we were scheduled to fly again. This time we were to strike an airplane parts factory in Leipzig, Germany, a target with a bad reputation. Our bomb load was six 500-pound GP (general purpose) bombs and four 500-pound incendiary bombs. The regular GPs would not detonate unless the fuse was hit. The firebombs would go off if hit anywhere. I sure hated to fly with those things. We were leading the low squadron again, and this was to be our position from now on. Our route into target and out was close to yesterday's, and so we had the same attention including flak and fighters. The fighters came in first at the tail and our tail gunner knocked one out. Then they flew around and came in at the nose. One came at us from a 12 o'clock high and did a slow roll while firing, never wavering. He passed right under us, upside down. I was shooting all the while and saw my tracers ricocheting off his armor plated belly. I do not know if any slugs went into him but I hoped at least, that I scared him. (He reminded me of a German version of Chuck Baker.) Jensen, our tail gunner, reported the plane he got was a twin engine Messerschmitt 110, and it blew up in his face.

When the last three days were history, we totaled our losses. Eight B-17s carrying eighty fine men had gone down. The returning planes carried many wounded back to base. In looking back over the years, I realize those three days with practically no sleep and very little to eat were the toughest ones I ever experienced.

MISSION 17

Boulogne, Germany

04 June 1944

The target today was the "Pill Box" coastal defenses on the French coast just north of the city of Boulogne. There were only twelve planes in the Group today but it turned out to be an easy mission. We each carried ten 500-pound general purpose bombs. We crossed the

---

When the last three days were history, we totaled our losses. Eight B-17s carrying eighty fine men had gone down. The returning planes carried many wounded back to base. In looking back over the years, I realize those three days with practically no sleep and very little to eat were the toughest ones I ever experienced.

English Channel, were over land only a brief time, dropped the bombs, and were on our way back to base. One of the other planes in our Group was not so lucky. It developed an oxygen fire in the upper turret while still over England. Nine of the crew was able to parachute to safety but the ball turret gunner burned to death.

MISSION 18

Abbeville, France

05 June 1944

We were briefed for Abbeville, France, not far into the Pas de Calais. The flak was extremely accurate. The number six plane in the lead squadron, just to our right, received a direct hit and exploded. A minute later, the number three position went down. The overcast was heavy, so we began to return to England. At Beachy Head, we aimed back to where we had been yesterday and gave them a second round of bombs.

Upon landing, we counted some twenty holes in *Bomboogie* including a large one that passed through Munroe's briefcase, which had been lying on his navigation table. Everything in the case was destroyed.

MISSION 19

D-Day

06 June 1944

Up at 3 a.m. this morning and were quite excited to know where we would be assisting in THE Landing on Normandy Beach by Liberation Forces. Our target was a crossroad of two main highways, in the center of Falaise. This was to be obliterated to prevent any German force from getting to the beachhead. I could look straight down at the Channel and see large ships firing towards the shore. But the weather was so lousy I could not see anything smaller than that. I could not see the target, so we turned around and took our bombs back to England. Bob Munroe, Navigator wrote in his diary "This is it." At briefing we were told of the plans for the Invasion. For the past week, we were able to anticipate the Invasion from

Up at 3 a.m. this morning and were quite excited to know where we would be assisting in THE Landing on Normandy Beach by Liberation Forces. Our target was a crossroad of two main highways, in the center of Falaise. This was to be obliterated to prevent any German force from getting to the beachhead.

seeing LSTs (Landing Ship Tanks) in the channel. At any rate "this was it" and we were eager with anticipation about seeing the big show from a ringside seat at 20,000 feet. However, 3 hours later our hopes were dashed, for over the channel and along the coast we were completely undercast. "It hurt to know we would not see the show." This mission was another "milk run." We saw no flak, no enemy planes, and dropped no bombs. Our efforts to assist in the landings were zero. We were back at our base in time for lunch and a nap.

Later in the day, the 390th sent another group to the target and this time they were able to drop their bombs.

MISSION 20

Nantes, France
07 June 1944

The mission today was another tactical one, a railroad bridge over the Loire River at Nantes, close to the Atlantic Coast. A strong Panzer (tank) force from the south was heading for the Normandy Beach and would need this crossing. We were told this was a 'Do or Die' thing. The sky was 7/10ths overcast, and we got ready to go several times before we got a clear shot at it. We had to destroy this bridge. Luck was with us and we got it on the first pass. The flak was heavy and accurate, and I hate to think what might have happened if we would have had to make multiple runs.

This was a late afternoon mission and we did not land until 10:30 pm. We found several more holes in *Bomboogie*! The next day photos proved we had knocked out the bridge.

To round out the day, we heard explosions around our base and realized we were being bombed. Our anti-aircraft gunners were blazing away at a Junkers-88 (a German twin engine bomber) while a Me-109 buzzed our runway. I was highly amused by the running around of many of our personnel in their long johns and bare feet looking for a place to hide. I was too tired to run and hide. We had flown four missions in four days, although they weren't too long or too stressful, I was really tired tonight. I just wanted to go to bed.

One evening about this time, a replacement crew was ushered into our barracks. The

A strong Panzer force from the south was heading for the Normandy Beach and would need this crossing. We were told this was a 'Do or Die' thing. The sky was 7/10ths overcast, and we got ready to go several times before we got a clear shot at it. We had to destroy this bridge. Luck was with us and we got it on the first pass. The flak was heavy and accurate.

pilot took one look at me and said, "Where's Munroe?" I said, "He's right there stretched out on that cot." It seems he was the officer back in Ardmore who was searching for Bob. His name was Dale Livingston. We all shook hands and laughed about that episode. We soon all were good friends and we see him at our reunions.

08 June 1944

Baker went to the hospital with tonsillitis and the crew got a couple of days off.

13 June 1944

In Baker's diary he says, "We went to London on a two-day pass. We didn't do anything out of the ordinary and didn't see anything of interest. We must have just slept for two days."

MISSION 21

Dinard-Pleurtuit, France

11 June 1944

Back to France again in order to strike a German air base out on the Brest Peninsula. We each carried three dozen bombs. These bombs were unique, weighing about 100 pounds and equipped with a special delayed action fuse. They were designed to detonate on contact, when tampered with, or anytime from one to 36 hours. This made the area inoperative since one could not predict when any one of the bombs would explode. On this mission we flew through solid clouds and bombed by Pathfinder Radar. Thus, it would have been impossible to evaluate the hits.

MISSION 22

Misburg, Germany

15 June 1944

Today was our first break from tactical bombing prior to D-Day. The target was an oil refinery at Misburg, a town near Hanover, Germany. Bombing was through 9/10th cloud cover, and once again we could not evaluate the results. I saw no enemy fighters and the flak appeared light. Both were rare, considering we were over the Fatherland.

MISSION 23

Hanover, Germany

18 June 1944

For some unknown reason we were awakened before midnight to fly. What were they thinking? We had just gone to bed at 9:00 pm. The briefing was to an oil refinery in Hanover.

The weather information was poor and takeoff was into soup. We broke out of the clouds only to find the undercast starting to rise. We kept climbing to stay on top of it. The command pilot was forced to change the aim from the factory to the City Center. By the time we arrived, our altitude was 30,000 feet, and I noticed my fingertips and nails had turned blue due to lack of oxygen in my blood. I became concerned about the pilots and wondered how they were functioning.

The flak was heavy but fortunately mostly remained below us by about 1,000 feet. That was OK by me.

We missed our target by eight miles. Upon returning to base it was determined that the strain of taking overloaded planes to 30,000 ft. resulted in most engines in the Group having to be replaced.

MISSION 24
Basdorf, Germany
21 June 1944

The 390th put up two groups today. One was to bomb in Poland, and then go on to land in Russia. Ours was a diversionary mission to Berlin. The weather was bad and our group leader could not decide which alternate target to bomb, and while he was deciding, we were getting the daylights shot out of us. The decision was finally made to hit a motor works at nearby Basdorf, though there were several other targets in the area.

We saw no German fighters but the flak was as accurate and heavy as I had experienced to date. I had dropped the load and was sitting with my elbows on my knees watching the bombs fall. Suddenly my left arm disappeared. Munroe was shaking and yelling, "Are you OK? Are you OK?" I finally got my act together and realized my arm had been knocked behind me. When I brought it back around, I could not feel anything. There was no blood but there was a hole in my left sleeve. I looked to the right and spotted an opening in the plexiglas. Something had come through and struck my arm. I started peeling off my upper clothing one by one (no small endeavor). When I got the shirt off, I found a cube of 88-mm shell resting on my arm. It had traveled through the glass and through six layers of clothing before it stopped.

No skin had been broken but the following morning, I had a 6-inch diameter bruise on my forearm. The bruise was centered with a red burn spot. Quote from Chuck Baker's diary, "Ordel was hit by a piece of white hot, screaming flak." Boy, am I glad it really had not been like that.

Double bummer for the day happened when we arrived back at the base. We were advised that the required number of missions to be flown had been increased from thirty to thirty-five.

Bomboogie was found to need a new wing, so we wished we might get a few days rest.

Area 05 in the foothills of the French Alps

MISSION 25

Paris-St. Ouen, France

22 June 1944

We dressed for Paris today, but no one wore a beret. Our target was an oil storage depot along the Seine River, south of Paris. The weather was bright and sunny. I could look down into the heart of downtown Paris. It was a fabulous sight, one I never ever expected to have. There was plenty of flak and we lost one B-17 to it. Coming out, we flew over Fontainebleau and got a lot more flak. I was humming "I Bombed Paris in the Springtime," and Munroe said, "I hope it is 'The Last Time I See Paris.'" (Popular tunes at this time were "I love Paris in the Springtime" and "The Last Time I Saw Paris").

Munroe and I were both promoted to First Lieutenant today. Gilmore got his two weeks ago and I'm not sure when Baker got his. I really liked the wording of the Official Order which stated "By command of General Eisenhower" and I did not realize he knew me!

It was nice to replace the gold bars with silver ones, but the best part of it was a magnanimous increase in pay. Instead of $225.00 we would now be getting $250.00 per month. That was almost $8.50 a day.

Notice the smoke in lower right to mark the target area.

MISSION 26

Area 05

28 June 1944

Our load for today was supplies for the Maquis, the Free French Underground. There were only eleven planes in this operation and we each carried twelve containers holding about 500 pounds of machine guns, bazookas, rifles, and ammo. This was to supply about 300 men.

We flew over Omaha Beach at 16,000 feet heading south toward Chartres and then descended to 300 ft. We had a passenger with us in the plane's nose, an intelligence captain, but I questioned that. We were over Chartres, and getting shot at as he was admiring the flak. I found his flak helmet on the floor, and slapped it on his head. This was his first mission, so I guess he could be excused. We flew on south, descending all the way to an area in the foothills of the French Alps, watching for a flat field with three fires arranged in a triangle. We found it OK, and parachuted our loads out the bomb bays. They hit the ground about the time the chutes were fully opened. We came around and saw the last of the containers being dragged into the woods with everyone there waving at us. I never would have believed I would have dropped a load from a B-17 at an altitude of 300 feet. We climbed back up to 16,000 feet and returned to base.

The Resistance had radioed back to England before we got there, thanking us for the supplies. This was the only mission I flew that gave me a sense of great satisfaction.

We learned after the war, that sometime later these Frenchmen engaged a unit of highly trained German troops and were wiped out.

MISSION 27
Bohlen, Germany
29 June 1944

Today we were briefed for a synthetic oil factory at Bohlen, Germany, which was a few miles south of Leipzig. We had been briefed for this target several times before but the missions had always been scrubbed. We knew this was a dangerous location and it surely lived up to its reputation. The weather was nice and the plant was easily located. We had a half-hearted fighter attack, but the flak was so bad they didn't hang around and risk being shot down by their own flak.

We got more flak hits today than any previous mission. One piece came through the nose pexiglas, through my gun sight barely missing my head, passed through three bulkheads, and out the rear of the plane. Another came just above Munroe's head, through a heater in the cockpit, through a can, and lodged in Gilmore's boot. Another one came up through the floor of the nose. Upon landing, we counted 40 holes in the wings. There were two pieces of flak about 7" long in a wing, but the worst was a hit in the number one fuel tank. It lost no gas, as it had been used up earlier. I could not believe none of us had been struck.

One of our planes ditched over the North Sea, and the crew was rescued by an Allied air-sea rescue plane. The Allied plane was spotted and fired at by a German plane, killing two of the rescued passengers.

The mission to Bohlen was as rough as they come, but we had no crew casualties. *Bomboogie* required two new wings and four new engines.

RELAX, REST AND RECREATION
Bournmouth, United Kingdom
30 June 1944

A day we had been looking forward to for a long time had finally arrived. We got a ten-day pass and were headed for the "flak house." Someone up there realized our crew had seen too many "rockets, red glare, and bombs bursting in air." In order to keep us out of the "loony bin," they had arranged for us to visit the Red Cross R&R (rest, relaxation, recreation, recuperation, etc.) facility at the famous seaside resort at Bournmouth, on the English Channel. All of us went, the four officers and the six enlisted men.

We left early the next morning, but missed our train and had to wait three hours for the next one. That was probably the best wait of our lives, because when we arrived at our hotel in London, we were told we had dodged a pilotless German V-1 aircraft about two hours before we got there. It hit the top floors where the Americans were always lodged. We called them "buzz bombs" and the British called them "doodle bugs." They carried a thousand pounds

Left to right: Bob Munroe, Art Ordel, Gillie Gilmore in Bournmouth. Picture by Chuck Baker

of explosives, flew 400 mph, ran out of fuel right over London, and dropped like streamlined bricks. They had no military value, and were only meant to terrorize citizens. No doubt, we would have been in it and received full benefit of the blast. We had to find another hotel and were happy to leave next morning with London behind us.

Our hotel in Bournmouth, The Ambassador Cliff, was perched high above the Channel and we could look down at the beach, and see all kinds of barriers, traps, barbed wire, etc., and I suspect Normandy Beach looked much the same before D-Day.

Our gunners were billeted in the Granville Court Hotel about a block away. These hotels had been taken over and were operated by the American Red Cross, which were quite nice and the food was good.

I thought that we would lay about this place for the week with nothing to do but rest and relax. The Social Director had other ideas; her job was to keep us busy. The first day, she sent us horseback riding. I drew a horse that kept throwing his head back wanting to bite me. Going away from the stable, the four critters could hardly be made to move, but when we turned around it looked like "derby day" until we got back. Another day, we were to try golfing on a dark and overcast day and when we got there and I saw the unkempt conditions of the course, I was ready to go back to the hotel. I was out-voted, so we rented the golf clubs, bought a bucket of well-used, expensive balls and sallied forth. The rough was rough, the weeds were tall, and the greens were green, which was the only nice thing one could say about them. It started to drizzle and we began losing balls in the tall grass and before long, we were down to only one ball. We took turns using it, until it too disappeared, but by then we were soaking wet and glad to call it quits.

We escaped on a couple of occasions, wandering around town, window-shopping. The Granville Court was practically vacant and that Red Cross director invited us over there two or three times to dine with the rest of our crew, and that was most enjoyable.

In the evenings at our hotel, they always had a small combo to provide music and there were always a bunch of girls present for us to meet. One evening, the director introduced Baker and me to a pair of sisters, one in a W.A.A.F. (Women Army Air Force) uniform, and the other in civvies (civilian clothing). We invited them to dance, but they said it was too crowded and they would rather have us teach them an American card game, named poker, so we played cards. After a while, an older woman came over to watch and one of the girls looked up and said "Hello, Mama." At 9:00, all the girls had to leave, but a few minutes later one of them came back in and said "Mama wants you to come to our house next evening for a meal." We asked how to get there, and she described a zigzag ride by bus. We didn't think we could handle that, so she said we should be at the hotel and she would pick us up the next evening and she would navigate the bus as a couple of transfers were required.

We had a delightful time. The meal was probably sumptuous to their standards. It included eggs and a cake made with "dirty" flour. (White flour was not available in England during the war.) They were admirers of Marion Anderson and had a collection of her records, which they played on a crank-up phonograph. I casually mentioned that today was July 4 and then they said, "So what?" Then we had to explain that this was the day we celebrated our independence from the oppressive British rule. They were good sports and were vigorous in their defense of their nation when we described the horrors of the Boston Massacre and other such American incidents. It was an evening to remember, and one of the few times we visited in a British home.

Our stay in Bournmouth ended all too quickly. We spent ten days in a Rest Home and got no rest but I felt much better for it. I certainly was not crazy about getting back to the flying routine of missions.

MISSION 28

Munich, Germany
11 July 1944

Munich, Germany, the mission today was to be dreaded. Flak was legendary and the city was always heavily defended. The aiming point was the railroad yards but anywhere inside the city limits would be accepted as good bombing.

The BMW plant down there was a major producer of military equipment and I hoped it would receive a few of the eggs we dropped. The flak was heavy but most of it was below the plane. We released our bombs and headed home. The Alps were a few miles over on our left. What a sight!

A short time after "Bombs Away" the plane flying #2 in the lead squadron had a hit in the cockpit and evidently both pilots were immobilized. The out-of-control plane veered off to the left, hit the tail of the #1 plane, and then came down barely missing our plane. I did not see any of this until it appeared below us in the eleven o'clock position going straight down. I saw no parachutes, and when it hit the ground it produced a huge fire ball creating many acres of devastation.

MISSION 29

Munich, Germany

13 July 1944

For a second day in a row the Group went to Munich. It was an all-out effort using 1,200 B-17s and B-24s to bomb the city. After three days of pounding by these bombers, it was a wonder that anything was still standing down there.

The mission was pretty much the same as the one on the same route, same bomb load, and same target. The main difference was that the Group lost a B-17 that day.

This was the longest mission we had EVER flown.

MISSION 30

Schweinfurt, Germany

19 July 1944

A ball bearing factory at Schweinfurt, Germany, was the second most dreaded place that I did not want to fly, with Berlin being number one. Schweinfurt was on the south end of the Ruhr Valley and only by very good navigation and zigzagging around flak concentrations, did we keep from getting our tails shot off.

On the bomb run, we watched the group ahead of us get pounded. As we got closer another group showed up, flying parallel to us. This must have confused the flak gunners below us because most of their stuff exploded between us.

After we left the target we took more flak, including some green smoke which I had never seen before.

We lost another B-17 this day.

If the requirement of thirty missions had not been increased to thirty-five, this one would have been our last. Instead, there are five more to go.

We were told today was to be our last mission in Bomboogie, and she would be assigned to a new crew. She got us through some tough times, but always brought us home. Bomboogie had a most remarkable life. She flew 94 missions, almost a record for our Group, and only one time had a crewman been wounded. After the war, she went back to the US and was mothballed in Kingman, Arizona. Many years later she was chopped up, and recycled into a new career, probably beer cans or siding for a mobile home. The average life of a B-17 flying with the 390th was 32 missions. As of this day, Bomboogie had flown 55 missions.

Getting a brand new plane for this mission surprised us. It was a nice shiny, silver B-17G, fresh from the factory in the US. Someone had painted the name "Sweetheart of the Pas de Calaias" on it with big letters. This was our fourth plane, and we never had the opportunity to name any one of them. It was nice to have the new one, but I kind of missed Bomboogie.

MISSION 31

Villedeau-Les-Poeles, France

24 July 1944

Our target today was most unusual. It was near St. Lo, and 1,500 four-engine and two-engine bombers were to bomb on a six-mile-square area held by the Germans.

After we finished, the Allied Troops were to pour in on a wide front and take possession. We flew in over Normandy beachhead but the clouds obscured our target and we were notified to bomb a railway depot at Villedeau-Les-Poeles. We bombed from 14, 000 feet, which was our lowest altitude for a mission so far.

Except for flying our new plane, this was not a very exciting day.

MISSION 32

St. Lo, France

25 July 1944

We were briefed today to repeat yesterday's briefed target. Everything was to be the same. We had more flak than yesterday and to make it more interesting, we also had rockets aimed at us. We had to pull up a bit to pass over ten men in parachutes from the group in front of us. We felt that our bombing was accurate but reports later said one group dropped short and many Americans were killed. Friendly fire can kill just as surely as enemy fire.

The following article written by Ernie Pyle appeared in *Stars and Stripes* newspaper. It describes very vividly and accurately our July 25th mission to St. Lo:

> Our "front lines" were marked by long stripes of colored cloth laid on the ground, and with colored smoke to guide our airmen during the mass bombing that preceded our breakout from the German ring that held us to the Normandy beachhead.
>
> The dive-bombers hit just right. We stood in the barnyard of a French farm, and watched them barrel nearly straight out down out of the sky. They were bombing about a half-mile ahead of where we stood. They flew in groups, diving from every direction, perfectly tuned, one right after another. Everywhere you stood, separate groups of planes were on the way down or on the way back up or slanting over our heads waiting their turn. The air was full of sharp and distinct sounds of cracking bombs and heavy rips of the planes' machine-guns, and splitting screams of diving wings.
>
> And then a new sound gradually droned into our ears. The sound was deep and all encompassing with no notes in it, just a faraway surge of doom. They came from directly behind us, and at first they were the merest dots in the sky. You could see clots of them against the far heavens, too tiny to count individually; they came on with terrible slowness. They came in flights of six—three flights to a group. And the groups stretch out across the sky, they came in "families" of about 70 planes each.

Maybe these giant waves were two miles apart, maybe ten miles. I do not know, but I do know that they came in constant procession, and I thought it would never end. What the Germans must have thought is beyond comprehension. Their march across the sky was slow and steady. I've never known a storm or machine, or any resolve of man that had about it the aura of such ghastly relentlessness. You have the feeling that even had God appeared beseechingly before them in the sky with palms outward to persuade them back they would not have had within them the power to turn from their irresistible course.

I stood with a little group of men ranging from colonels to privates in back of some farmhouse. Slit trenches were all around the edges of the farmyard, and a dugout with a tin roof was nearby, but we were so fascinated by the spectacle overhead that it never occurred to us that we might need the foxholes.

The first huge flight passed directly over our farmyard, and the others followed. We spread our feet and leaned far back trying to look straight up until our steel helmets fell off. We'd cup out fingers around our eyes like the field glasses for a clearer view, and then the bombs came.

They began ahead of us as a crackle of popcorn, and almost instantly swelled into monstrous fury of noises that seemed to destroy the whole world ahead of us. From then on, for an hour and a half that had in it the agonies of centuries, the bombs came down. A wall of smoke and dust erected by them grew high in the sky. It filtered along the ground, back through our own orchard; it sifted all around us and into our noses. The bright day grew slowly dark from it.

The Germans began to shoot heavy high ack-ack. Great black puffs of it by the score speckled the sky until it was hard to distinguish the planes from the smoke puffs.

And then someone shouted that one of the planes was smoking. Yes, we could all see it. A long faint line of black smoke stretched for a mile behind one of them, and as we watched there was a gigantic sweep of flames over the plane from nose to tail. It disappeared in flames and it slanted slowly down, and banked around sky in great curves, this way and that way, and rhythmically and gracefully as in a slow-motion waltz. Then suddenly it seemed to change its mind, and it swept upward, steeper and steeper and ever slower until it seemed poised motionless on its own black pillar of smoke. And just as slowly, it turned over and dived for the earth—a folded spearhead on the straight black shaft of its own creation, and it disappeared behind the trees.

But before it was done, there were more cries of "There's another one smoking, and there's a third one now."

Chutes came out of some of the planes; out of some came no chutes at all. One of the white silk caught on the tail of a plane. The men with binoculars could see him fighting to get loose until the flames swept over him, and then a small black dot fell through all alone.

And all the time the great flat ceiling of the sky roofed by all the others that did not go down, plowing their way forward as if there were no turmoil in the world. Nothing deviated them in the slightest. They stalked on slowly and with the dreadful pall of sound as though they were seeing something at a great distance, and nothing existed between them.

—Written by Ernie Pyle in *Stars and Stripes*

This mission was a great success. We opened a path for our American troops and they poured through, liberating a large area of Normandy.

26 July 1944

Our crew was given a two-day pass to London and when we returned to the base, Jimmy Stewart, our tail gunner, was unaccounted for. The other gunners said they had no idea of his whereabouts, so he was declared AWOL.

Later we learned he had been "dating" a French girl in London. She had told him as soon as Paris was liberated she was going home and wanted him to go along. The dummy must have forgotten he had only three more missions to fly and he had a young wife waiting back in Mississippi.

Today the four officers and the three sergeant gunners who still had three missions to fly, were notified that we would be awarded the Distinguished Flying Cross. What a surprise! We had been together since Ardmore, and I couldn't think of any really heroic actions by any of us. We just flew the plane, shot at German planes, navigated, and dropped bombs like all the other crews. We didn't look, act, or feel like movie heroes.

No John Wayne or Errol Flynn in this bunch. Between the time we received our Air Medal and carried out our last mission, we each had been awarded four Oak Leaf Clusters to the Air Medal and three battle stars on our ETO medal.

At the time, I was not impressed by these awards, but as the years have passed, I have come to appreciate them.

I give all the credit to Gilmore and Baker for their expertise in piloting the plane and getting us all back to base every time in one piece. The rest of us just had the benefit of flying with them.

MISSION 33

Munich, Germany
31 July 1944

Damn! Munich again. I was getting sick and tired of the long haul down to southern Germany. The briefing was identical to the last two times we went there. However, as we started on the bomb run, we got reports of intense fighter opposition over the target. The Wing commander ordered our three groups to form one unit and bomb as such. The result was 54 planes coming together to deliver 135 tons of high explosives simultaneously through the 100% cloud cover. I could not imagine the catastrophe on the ground. We lost no planes that day, possibly due to tight formation. Flying back to England we admired the beautiful Alps Mountains as we passed by.

Arriving back at 6:00 p.m. we were a very, very weary crew.

Other Thoughts

I never had any compunction about bombing the Germans. They started this thing and supported Hitler and his policies from day one and right up to the end. Most of them thought the only thing Hitler did wrong was to lose the war. Jesus, in his "Sermon on the Mount," said "Blessed are the Peacemakers." I still believe we were the Peacemakers.

MISSION 34

Harburg, Germany

04 August 1944

We were briefed this morning for a trip to Harburg, Germany, just a short distance from the sister city, Hamburg. These are at the north end of the Elbe River, where it empties into the North Sea. The target was an oil refinery. The bomb load was twenty 250-pound bombs, something new. The weatherman was completely off the mark. At takeoff we flew through solid overcast and when we broke out, it took us three hours to get the formation assembled. We were over water, and came onto the target from the sea. As we approached land, we could see those black bursts of flak awaiting us. It was intense and very accurate, so much so, that our bombing was poor. We flew past Hamburg, which had been visited the night before by the RAF. Our altitude was 25,000 feet and the smoke from the burning city was at least 15,000 feet above us. We lost no planes, but those planes that landed that evening were a bunch of wrecks. Every one of our planes had been seriously damaged.

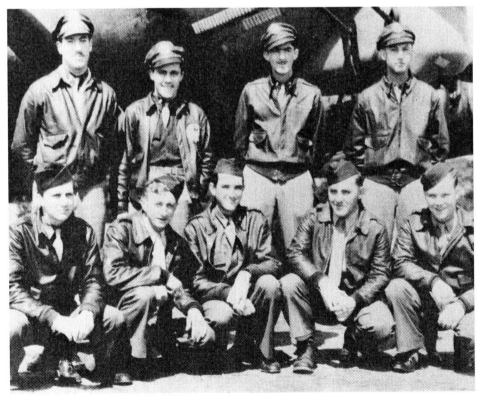

Taken after our last Mission: 390th Bomb Group stationed at Framlingham England, August 1944.
Back row: Charles Baker, Co-Pilot; Bob Munroe, Navigator; Bob Gilmore, Pilot; Art Ordel, Bombardier.
Front row: Charles Wittleder, Waist Gunner; Jerry Maisch, Radioman; Fred Anderson, Ball Turret; Raymond Jankowski, Waist Gunner; Robert Walters, Top Turret.

MISSION 35

St. Sylvan, France
08 August 1944

I had not been sleeping very well the past couple of nights, sweating out our LAST MIS-SION. We were called to fly again this morning and I hopped out as usual.

I was anxious to know where we would be going. When the briefing officer pulled back the curtain, I thought how nice, they gave us a "milk run." The target was St. Sylvain, France, just south of the beachhead and the English Channel. We would bomb in an area much as we did at St. Lo, in order to open a gap for the British troops at Caen, to pour though. Fog covered the base runways and takeoff would be by instrument. We broke out of the clouds at 2,500 ft into brilliant sunshine. Our planes made the formation and we crossed the Channel, climbing toward Cherbourg, where we turned eastward.

Evidently, the Germans heard we were coming, and the sky turned black. We were at 12,000 feet, about half of our usual altitude. I never saw so much flak as we had that day and never more accurate. To make it worse, I could look out my left window, and see the peaceful Channel sparkling in the sunshine. I dropped my bombs, and we turned toward the Channel, and looked for a clear path but the flak stayed with us. We finally flew over water, out of the flak. Suddenly jubilation and pandemonium broke out in the rear of the plane. Bob and I hugged, and then I crawled up to the cockpit to congratulate the pilots. All the gunners were firing their guns and the plane was shaking, like it was going to fall apart. In a minute or so Gilly said he was going back to talk to the crew.

I slipped into Gilly's seat to talk to Chuck, and the next thing I knew he too went back to talk to the crew. There I was alone with the controls, leading a Squadron of B-17s across the English Channel. There were five more planes following me. If I went down, killing sixty men and destroying six B-17s, I bet they would make me donate more than ten pounds to the Red Cross. I do not know how long I sat there, but I kept my eyes glued on the instrument panel holding the compass bearing, the airspeed, and altitude exactly where Baker had left them.

The two pilots, the navigator, and the six gunners kept whooping it up in the back of the plane. Then for some reason, Gilmore began to wonder who was flying the plane. I tried to look cool as he stormed back to the cockpit to reclaim his seat.

Sadly, upon landing, we learned the co-pilot in the lead ship was killed when a piece of flak struck him in the forehead the night of 08 August 1944.

I slept harder than I had any time in the last three and a half months.

CHAPTER 11

Post Operations

Framglingham, England

10 August–15 December 1944

I probably slept late on August 10, and when I awoke, I said, "Now what?" I had accomplished what I had been trained for and what I had hoped for. We flew our thirty-five missions with no one killed or injured, we never saw any blood, and we escaped bailing out, ditching, or becoming prisoners of war. I doubt that many other crews got by as easily as we did. We flew several "milk runs," but just as many really tough ones, too. The 390th Bomb Group flew a total of 301, and we were on thirty-five of these. The Group lost 145 B-17s missing in action, and seventeen more that crashed in England or in liberated areas of the continent. The Group lost twenty-three B-17s in missions that they were on. We flew ours in about three and a half months or about ten missions a month. There were only five times when the Group lost more planes than on our Magdeburg mission.

Our crew was told we had inherited "lucky cots" when we arrived at the 390th back in April. Little did they know. According to Baker's diary, fourteen crews in our barracks were lost while we were operational, and we were the only ones in that three and a half months period to complete our required thirty-five missions and be sent home. I cannot verify the fourteen downed crews and I cannot remember a single other crew finishing up while we were there.

During our operational weeks, we talked about what we would do after the war, and now I had to make a decision. Gilmore said he wanted to go home to get married. Bob Munroe was eager to get back to the States, as his wife Jerri, was expecting a baby. Bucky Walter and Maisch both just wanted to go home. Baker was non-committal. Fred Anderson didn't know what he wanted to do, and neither did I. Within a couple of days, Baker decided to stay in England and try to become a fighter pilot. He had talked with our "brass," and was told that if we wanted to stay, we could have a non-combat flying job and a ground position as well. I thought it over, and as I had no pressing reason to go home, I accepted that deal. When Fred heard of our plans, he said he would stay, too. So it was decided, that of the seven of us who had been together since Ardmore, four would go back to the States and three would stay in England. For our ground job, Chuck was assigned to the parachute department and I was assigned to air-sea rescue, which meant the life raft and "Mae West" shop. I cannot remember where Fred was assigned.

I doubt that Baker ever showed his face in the parachute department but I spent a good bit of time messing around the life raft shop. There were two 5-man life rafts on a B-17, plus ten one-man rafts and ten Mae Wests. The emergency food and canned water on the 5-man rafts had to be replaced every so often. The shop had a jeep and that took my eye. I grabbed the jeep, drove it up and down the runways, around the parked planes, and taught myself to drive. Of course, it had a stick shift. I came into the Air Corps, having never been in an airplane and not knowing how to drive. Well, I could not say that anymore.

There was not any rush about sending the ones going home on their way. We all went to London together a couple of times before they left Station 153. I think it was a week or two into our retirement, when Gilmore got a call to come see the Squadron Commander. The Colonel explained that a top-secret mission was coming up and he needed our experience to lead the low squadron in the slot we filled on our last twenty or so. He could not say anything about it, but we would all get a DFC if we went. He told Gillie to get the seven of us to meet and talk it over. This we did, we agreed to a secret ballot, and we would all go along with the majority. He gave each of us a paper and told us to write Yes or No on it. We each voted, and folded the paper and put it in his hat. He shook it and dumped it on the bed. The vote was one Yes and six No votes. Baker immediately wanted to know what was wrong with us, because this would be a great opportunity to see some new country. Our Group had previously been on two shuttles and we guessed that was what this one was. The mission would bomb a target deep into Germany, too deep to get back to England, but would go on to Russia and land. They would spend that night there, gas up and get a refill on bombs, and then head for Italy, bombing in Bulgaria, or Romania on the way. They would reload everything there, and head back for England, bombing a target in France or Germany on the way. The crews would get credit for three missions.

Gilmore went back to the Colonel, gave the results of the vote, and told him we each already had a DFC. The Colonel said he really needed us and to go back and vote again and we would be awarded an Oak Leaf Cluster to our DFC. To make a long story short, we voted again with the result of six to one. The Colonel said he was disappointed but that would be the end of it.

The missions finally took place on September 18-19 to Warsaw, Poland and Szlonock,

Hungary. The Russians had broken through the German lines in Russia, and they were battling their way eastward toward Berlin. The Polish people expected them to continue on so, they rose up against the Germans and had taken back 1/3 of Warsaw, but were badly in need of supplies. A couple of groups of B-17s from England brought these supplies to help the beleaguered city. The weather information the Group had was bad, and most of the supplies floated into the German-held part of the city. When the Russians heard the Polish were battling the Germans, they halted their advance about thirty miles east of Warsaw and waited until the Germans and Polish had killed as many of each other as possible. When the rebellion died down, they resumed their advance.

Our Group lost one B-17 over Warsaw and shortly after landing in Russia, a force of German planes bombed them and we lost several of our bombers parked on the ground, but none of our crews.

Thirty or forty years after the war, the Polish government awarded a medal to every American who participated in these missions. I believe it was called the Polish Home Cross. When Chuck Baker heard about this, he said he would have been a Polish War Hero if we all hadn't chickened out back in 1944. Sometime later, the Russians also awarded a medal to the Americans who took part in the missions.

During my combat flying period, I missed a lot of meals, and did not eat much when I did go to the mess hall. I weighed about 150 pounds when I arrived in England, and by the time I finished my missions, I was down to 125 pounds. I realized that I looked like a scarecrow, and made a conscious effort to gain weight. By the time I left England, I was back up to 150 pounds and most of that, I believe, was because of that ersatz eggnog made of powdered eggs, powdered milk with sugar and vanilla flavoring.

Looking back at our mess hall offerings, I believe everything that we ate, except that cold cereal, came from the USA. Every bit of it came out of a box or a can.

Baker and I were left pretty much to our own devices. Our flying job was put upon us, but did not seem like work. Our duty was to "slow time" B-17s which had sustained major damage and repairs. We were to check them out by flying up to 20,000 feet for at least an hour to evaluate their worthiness. Baker became the Crew Commander. I was the Navigator, and a Co-pilot and enlisted Crew Chief were provided. As far as I know, we had no itinerary and we just flew up there looking for excitement. Chuck liked to find a British bomber and fly formation with him. The poor Brit would be horrified when Chuck tried to stick his wing in the other plane's window. He probably thought that crazy Yank was trying to kill him.

If Chuck spotted a fighter plane, he tried to get it into a dogfight with him. After Baker made a pass or two at him, he might get into the game, and try to get on our tail. Chuck would get our plane moving as fast as he could, and if the other pilot came up on us, Chuck would suddenly cut the throttle, and go into a steep diving turn. Since the fighter could not turn as tight as we could, he would go zooming straight ahead. If the other pilot wanted to do it again, it took him five or ten minutes to turn around and get back at us.

When Chuck said the B-17 was ready for operations again, there was no doubt in anyone's mind that it was ready. He could lose three or four thousand feet in one of those diving turns, and it never would get that much stress again.

Shortly before our four crew mates departed for the States, there was as an awards ceremony for us and another dozen or two men were given their DFC awards. All seven of us now had the DFC medal and an Air Medal with four Oak Leaf Clusters. We were entitled to wear the Europe, Africa, Middle East ribbon (we called it the ETO ribbon) with three battle stars on it. These stars were for the battles of Germany, France and Normandy. We were also allowed to wear the North American Defense ribbon and the Victory Medal, which was authorized. I had a Good Conduct ribbon, awarded when I was a cadet. The medals for these last four ribbons were not actually issued until about ten years after the war. The ETO ribbon, which we wore, irked the British people. They could not understand why anyone should get a medal for being in England.

The DFCs were pinned on us by Colonel Edgar Witten who had been our Commanding Officer. Sad to say, a week or so later he was accidently killed. He was learning to fly a P-47 and something went wrong, and he bailed out of the plane at a very low altitude and hit the ground before his chute opened. Everyone wanted to be a hot shot fighter pilot.

At every opportunity, Baker would go to a fighter base, and try to get checked out in a P-51 or P-47. He was rebuffed each time, but he was not deterred and kept visiting these bases in hopes that one of them would take him. It seems that the commanding officers of

1st Lieutenants lined up to receive their Awards of Distinguished Flying Cross awarded by Colonel Edgar Witten. Shown: Gillie is the 2nd and Art is the 4th from the left.

fighter groups had a low opinion of B-17 pilots. Chuck did have one happy experience at one of those bases. He met one of his old buddies from pilot school, and this guy took him out to the flight line and told Baker to takeoff in a P-51. I do not know how long he was up, but he was one happy man when he arrived back at the 390th that evening. Everyone wanted to be a fighter pilot.

During the first year of flying in England, the Eighth Air Force suffered heavy losses due to overwhelming power of the Luftwaffe. Our fighter planes did not have the range to escort the heavy bombers very deep into Germany. The bombers were over the Continent as much as five or six hours and our fighters could not stay with them much more than half of that time, leaving bombers to the tender mercies of the German Air Force.

Eventually, the Eighth Air Force developed expendable wing tanks and a plane to match the Germans. The P-51 was a good plane but grossly underpowered. Negotiations with the British finally put Rolls-Royce Merlin engines in the P-51, and with the added fuel capacity, it could fly to Berlin and beyond. All this came together about the time my crew arrived over there. When we went to Berlin or Munich or some other distant target, we had three sets of escorts. The first would meet us as we got over land, and stayed with us until we started the bomb run. On the way in, they zigzagged above us, watching out for German planes, or "bandits" as we called them. If they saw or heard of any, they would drop their wing tanks and join the battle. By the time we started the bomb run, they would be low on fuel and head back to home base. The second group would meet us as we started on the bomb run and stay with us over the target and as we were regrouping after "bombs away." They would generally be with us an hour or so. The third shift would join us at this time and take us back to England. They all flew in flights of four planes, and it was kind of exciting to see them drop their fuel tanks and high-tail it to where the action was. This is the way it was planned on paper but it did not always work out that way. Frequently they were early or late, and left gaps in the coverage, and sometimes they could not find us as all. On our mission to Magdeburg, they did not show up over the target, so we were unescorted and the Luftwaffe shot down five B-17s in our Group.

On September 2, as part of our slow time jobs, we flew Gilmore, Munroe, Maisch and Walters to an airfield near Liverpool where they would embark for the USA. It was a sad ending of a good crew. I never laid eyes on Gilmore or the two gunners again, and it was 39 years later before Baker, Munroe and I were together again.

I do not know if it was the wing headquarters of Third Bomb Division headquarters, and I cannot remember the location, but there was a meeting there of air-sea rescue people. Captain Morgan, personnel equipment officer who was more or less my boss now, told me that I would be representing him at the meeting. A private driving a jeep was my chauffeur, and it probably took an hour to drive to the site. The building was a beautiful old mansion on a large well-manicured estate. I cannot remember the agenda, how long it lasted, if we had lunch, or any details about the meeting. I do not think I even gave a report to Captain Morgan.

On our return, the private asked me if we could stop at some friends' for a few minutes, and I said okay. The friends were an old couple whom he had met some time ago and he more or less adopted them. Their residence was 400 years old; the kitchen was about seven feet by nine feet with a fireplace and a dirt floor. The living room, ten feet by ten feet, was a step up and had a wood floor. There was a ladder on one wall leading up to a bedroom. The same family had owned the house since it had been built. I guess that they were living in the same manner as their 16th-century ancestors. The couple had a daughter who taught school in Jersey or Guernsey in the Channel Islands, but the couple had not heard from her in five years. The Germans took over the islands in 1939, and there was no outside communication for the residents. This couple raised most of their own food, using the seed, which they saved each year. The private told me he had his mother send a variety of seeds from America to them, and they were astounded at how good their garden was now. I really enjoyed talking with them, and when we left they gave six duck eggs to my driver, and three crabapples to me.

Back at the base, all was well with Baker and me. We flew about twice a week, and were on our own the rest of the time. I could go to the Officers Club, and find something to read. There was always the *Stars and Stripes* newspaper, *Yank* magazine, the *London Times* or maybe a paperback book. A radio tuned to the BBC was always on, and I could get some good recipes for cooking Brussels sprouts, or the scores of soccer matches, or doings of Parliament interspersed with classical music.

I discovered there was a "war room" where I could read some classified material, and other military stuff. The main attraction for me was a huge map of Europe, slightly smaller than the one in the briefing room, showing the battle lines on four fronts. One showed the liberated area in Normandy, one showed the advancing lines in southern France, one in Italy, and one showing the advance of the Russians in the east. These were adjusted daily as the war progressed.

I usually dropped by the life raft shop each day to see what was going on, and to give a hand if needed. I would also take the jeep for a spin around the runway if it was not being used.

I did not hang around the barracks much. Usually the crews were flying, and there were only cots there, but no chairs to sit on and it was unattractive. Twenty unmade beds, dark "blackout" curtains on the window, and an untidy floor. It was ok when the crews were there, but I liked the place best when I was tired and could sleep.

One reason I avoided the barracks was mail censoring. All outgoing mail had to be censored by an officer, and one lying around on a bed was a prime candidate. They generally got a gang of three, four or five of us, and brought us into the Orderly Room, where a stack of mail two feet high covering a table awaited, You were not allowed to mention anything about the missions, you could not mention any location except London and in fact, there was a list of "no-nos." We would quickly grab a big handful of letters and immediately discard anything written to a man or a Mrs. We wanted to read ones addressed to Miss. It was dull tedious work, but there were one or two gems in each pile. The envelopes were not sealed so we pulled the letter out, scanned it, and unless there was a flagrant violation, we sealed it and signed our name on the outside. If there was a real violation, we had a blank stamp with an inkpad and we blacked it out. When we were not too busy, I would find an extremely dull passage, I would black it out, hoping the recipient would think the writer was important enough to know some military secrets. One letter from a crew man to his wife stands out in my mind. He would be coming home shortly and she should take all the pretty pictures off the wall and hang them on the bedroom ceiling. That's all she would be looking at for the first couple of weeks that he was home.

When we first arrived at the 390th, we were visited by a British woman who said she would like to do our laundry for us, free of charge. All she wanted in return was any leftover soap we had. She knew crews would be shot down, leaving some bars of soap behind. We agreed to this and once a week she picked up our laundry and brought it back a day or two later. Our clothes were washed in Palmolive, Camay, Lifebuoy, and maybe even in Lava soap, but never in any real laundry soap. I did not have many washable garments except underwear, socks and an occasional khaki shirt, but the arrangement was very satisfactory.

I do not think I ever saw a dry-cleaning shop in England, but we solved this problem very simply. We took our woolens to the flight line, removed any metal ornamentation, got a clean bucket, filled it with 110-octane aviation gasoline, took it to an isolated spot and dunked the clothes in. We shook the garment once or twice, and it was dry enough to put back on. That probably was a dangerous procedure. One bit of static electricity might have sent me and my clothes to kingdom come.

On 6 September 1944, Colonel Joe Moller became the new group commander, and rivaled Colonel Edgar Witten in popularity. He was experienced and was accepted wholeheartedly by the Group. His predecessor was an old time spit and polish officer and did not seem to mesh with the younger squadron commanders. I recall him chastising us at briefing time for our sloppy attire and lack of military bearing. He was right, of course, but we thought winning the war took precedence over saluting and polished shoes. He could have taken Baker as an example. Around the base, Chuck never wore any insignia; no one knew what his rank was. He wore a sleeveless sweater with his shirt sleeves rolled up two times, and his right pants leg rolled up about three notches. This was in case he wanted to go bicycle riding. More than once, I heard Colonel Gemmel yell, "Baker, roll down that damn pants leg!"

My first meeting with Colonel Moller was at the entrance to the officers' club. He had an entourage of "brass" and was coming from one direction and I from the other. We arrived there simultaneously and the Colonel took the doorknob, opened the door and said, "After you, Lieutenant." I was surprised, but stepped inside, trailed by his staff. We met again thirty-nine years later at the first 390th reunion that I attended.

We were fortunate to have Baker on our crew, as he was the only one to own a camera. I think many servicemen in all theatres never had pictures of themselves in their military environment. I have a couple of pictures Baker made in Ardmore, and in England, and I have always treasured them. I often wished I had purchased film for him, but I always depended on him for that. Many of his photos are in this book.

After I had flown about half of my missions, I learned that our Group photography section had a camera that they would loan to take on missions. I decided to try it, and got one to take along with us. It was focused on infinity, and it was worthless for anything closer than 50 feet. They asked me to take pictures of any action, and to take a shot of a city any time that we flew close to it. This picture might help a lead crew find the target in case the bomb run was from that direction. After we finished our missions, Baker got chummy with those guys and they gave him several good aerial photos and he obtained many for me.

Early in October, Captain Morgan invited me to go on a trip with him to an RAF air-sea rescue station near Felixstowe on the east coast. He and I with Sgt Earl Clark as our jeep driver, departed early in the morning, arriving at the station as the sun was coming up. The mission for today was to ride a "high speed launch" well out into the North Sea, park it, and wait there to pick up any bomber crew that might have ditched into the water. We met the young officer in charge, and he introduced us to his ten-man crew. It was a beautiful ship, about the size of an American PT boat, with powerful engines and armed with a turret of four .30-caliber machine guns on the bow and a 20-mm cannon on the stern. The sea was calm, and we really cut the water as we sped out to our location. Once we got there, we had nothing to do, but wait for a call to rescue a crew. A couple of the men dropped lines into the water, hoping to catch something for supper, a few more busied themselves with their equipment or housekeeping, and two or three others took a snooze. The officer was proud of his command, and gave us a detailed tour of inspection and explanation. What took my eye was the 20-mm gun at the stern and I asked that gunner if there was any chance I could fire it. He must have been waiting for that, and in a minute, he had it all ready for me. He produced a five-gallon can and threw it overboard, and when it had floated about a hundred yards away, he told me to start firing. I took good aim, pressed my thumb on the trigger, and what a racket! It was much louder than our 50-caliber machine gun, and the ship shivered and hot grease from that gun started flying all around. I doubt if I fired more than half a second, but I churned the water all around that tin can, it kept floating. That gunner really had his gun greased up and it got hot immediately and really threw that stuff all over. He spent the next hour or two cleaning his gun and covering it with more grease. No lunch was served and the rest of the day was spent in boredom. Happily, we did not have to rescue anyone.

The sun had set by the time we returned to the pier, and as we did, the crew started milling around us and pushing, and it took me a minute to see they were trying to line us up. It seems the Royal Navy has a tradition called "splice the main brace." At the end of each voyage, the crew lined up and each man was given a shot of brandy. This RAF crew adopted that practice, and we being the visitors, were first in line to get that drink. The officer poured it out in a glass; each one of us swigged it down and handed the glass to the next man. This rum was to be used to revive fliers who had been in a wet life raft for a couple of days with their body temperature down to 67 degrees. It could have raised the dead. We had our supper in their mess hall, which featured curried billy goat. Somehow, we made it back to the 390th in the blackout, and agreed it had been a most unusual day.

Eight Months in England

Flying missions was a big thing for me, but being in a foreign country was another big experience. One day, we would be risking our lives over Europe, and the next day, we could be in London, being sightseeing tourists.

I did not have a lot of contact with the British people, but I liked the ones I met. Our presence there was known as "The Yankee Invasion of Britain." It was something they hadn't experienced in almost a thousand years, and it took them a while to get used to us. Good naturedly they said, "The trouble with the Yanks is they're overpaid, oversexed and over here." We answered with, "The problem with the British is they are underpaid, undersexed and under Eisenhower."

I believe they were grateful for our assistance in the war, but they shook their heads over some of our antics. According to their standards, we were over paid. My pay equaled a colonel in their army. Our private drew sixty dollars a month, their privates made the equivalent of fourteen dollars.

We were young, healthy, exuberant, and little concerned with tradition. The aircrews knew they could die tomorrow, so why not spend it today. We were also extravagant. The girls loved us, but the young men were jealous and hated us. The kids liked us. We had access to chewing gum and in London, they trailed us saying, "Got any gum, chum?" The newspapers took notice of this and pointed that "So much chewing gum had been spit out, that the pigeons in Trafalgar Square were beginning to lay golf balls."

Taxi cabs were a luxury for the people, but the Yanks rode them everywhere they went. The Brits' clothing was rationed and very plain. More than once, I had someone touch the sleeve of my blouse, just to feel the material. Their shoes were rough, and noisy. Ours had rubber soles and heels, and we walked quietly.

Almost all of my off-base experiences were in London. Someone told me the girls in London had two great desires. The first was to ride in a jeep and the second was to marry an American, but the jeep ride was number one. I thought the British were not as reserved as Americans but more open and friendly. We were traveling somewhere by bus and stopped for a while in the center of a small town. Parked there were three big truckloads of 15-year-old women in brown uniforms with ATS on the sleeve. They came over to where we were and soon were in lively conversation. Stupidly, I asked one what the ATS indicated, and she said Awfully Tough Stuff and another said Any Time Suits. I finally found it meant Auxiliary Territorial Service. These girls had been drafted to work on farms and were on their way to a job.

On one visit to London, as we walked passed a store, a man there was cussing out the Yanks. We asked him what the problem was, and he said a Yank had just passed by, eating a sandwich, and then threw it half-eaten on the sidewalk. The littering didn't bother him, but the wasted food was a sin. Food was scarce there and heavily rationed. Their flour, meat, tea, cooking oil, sugar, and other commodities were obtained only with ration tickets, and money. Most every home had window boxes on the sill, which held flowers before the war, now they were growing Brussels sprouts in them.

Munroe and I liked the theatre and went every time we could get tickets. In addition to one I mentioned before, I still have programs of three more shows I saw, including one called *Is Your Honeymoon Really Necessary?* (very forgettable), and two more which were really good; *Blithe Spirit* by Noel Coward, and *Arsenic and Old Lace*.

I stayed healthy while I was in England and did not require any type of medical attention, although we were constantly given shots. They told us that all kinds of diseases were running rampant through the Stalags (POW camps) and we needed to be immunized from all of them. It seemed that weekly, we got shots for black plague, white plague, green plague, orange plague, and many others I cannot remember. I did have a dental examination and it was determined I should have a tooth filled. I could not believe the antique the dentist brought out. It looked like a cross between a spinning wheel and a well drilling rig. The dentist stood on one leg and pedaled with the other. It developed about 33 RPMs. I believe the first person to be treated with that outfit probably was Gen. U.S. Grant at the Battle of Vicksburg.

Around the first of November, Baker and I were slow timing a B-17 at 20,000-ft. altitude and I looked down and about a thousand feet below us I saw a "Mosquito." This was a British multipurpose plane made of spruce plywood in Canada and then sent to England and fitted with two Rolls-Royce Merlin engines. It was the fastest propeller-driven aircraft in the ETO. It had a bomb bay and could carry two one-thousand-pound bombs, it could be fitted with machine guns for strafing, it could be rigged for aerial photography, and it could be used to gather meteorological data. It could do anything: it had a two-man crew, sitting side by side, a pilot and a bombardier-navigator.

I said, "Bake, there's a Mosquito below us" and he racked that B-17 practically upside down to see it. He pushed the throttles to the wall, and dived down to it and pulled up alongside to wave at the pilot. The pilot waved back and then he cut one of his engines, and feathered the propeller, not losing a bit of air speed. He did a slow roll around us, waved again, and took off like a scalded cat, still on one engine. Baker was chagrined, and said nothing until we got back to the barracks. There, he made his announcement. "Art, we're going to fly Mosquitos."

Chuck did his homework and found that the 8th Air Force had a reconnaissance group and were using Mosquitoes. He visited the base and got in to see the commanding officer. This colonel told Chuck that he was looking for a pilot and navigator who liked each other and had flown together for their combat missions, and he would train them to fly a Mosquito on reconnaissance missions, either gathering weather information or taking photographs. The colonel gave Chuck a handful of forms for us to sign, and he brought them back to the barracks, the happiest man in the world. He was so exuberant that I couldn't not sign them, and so we were off to a new adventure.

The next day, Chuck returned to the Mosquito outfit, with all the signed forms. The colonel read them over and at the bottom, he saw my signature, and asked Chuck who is this bombardier that signed here. Chuck said, "Ordel. He will be perfectly suited for the job." The colonel said, "I'm not going to have any damned bombardier lose one of my Mosquitoes over Europe and he tore up the papers. That colonel had a lot more sense than I did. I should have had my head examined for signing up in the first place.

Chuck was sorely disappointed over this episode, and coincidently within the next day or two, he got a letter from Donnabeth, his girlfriend. When the four of our crewmates left England to go home, we asked them to write our parents and tell them about some of our experiences. One of them wrote to Chuck's family, and when Donnabeth found out he could have come home, but didn't, she sat down and wrote him a letter. I didn't see the letter, but in essence, she said, "Come home immediately or don't ever come home."

Chuck came to me and said, "Art, I gotta go home." I was more than ready to go, so we checked with Fred and we went to see our squadron commander and requested a transfer back to the States.

One big reason that I decided to go home, was the war was progressing nicely for the allied troops. They had broken out of Normandy, liberated Paris and were moving closer to Germany every day. Everyone was pleased with this, and there were predictions the war should be over by Christmas. This led to rumors that we would all be sent directly to the Pacific area without a stop in the USA. That was terrible news.

We were briefed on the dos & don'ts of leaving England and I started packing my footlocker. Our luggage would be searched, they said and we were given a list of no-nos. At the top of the list were oxygen masks and firearms. I was more than happy to be rid of that hateful oxygen mask, but I had in my possession five .45-caliber automatic pistols, such as had been issued to us. One was my own but four belonged to guys who had given them to me to hold until they got back from a mission. They didn't return and I had their pistols. I really sweated over this, but chickened-out, and turned all five of them in. My footlocker had a lock on it, as it was shipped separately, and when it arrived at home more than a month later, the lock was intact and had not been opened. At this date 2015, those five pistols have a market value of around $4,000.

It took a week or so, but around the middle of the month, the three of us left station 153 and the 390th Bomb Group for a replacement depot, somewhere in England. We didn't go directly to Stone, but stayed in London for a night or two. I have very little recollections of this last visit, but I do remember staying at the Jules Club again and I have a dim memory of a room with four beds. Chuck and I occupied two of them, one was vacant and the other held a guy who had the worst snore I've ever encountered. We tried to wake him without success, and that horrible sound continued all night long.

We took a train from Waterloo Station and in a couple of hours we were at Stone. I believe we were there almost two weeks. There wasn't much to do, but we had a couple of USOs show up to visit us there during our stay. I also remember we had our Thanksgiving Day dinner there. A year ago, I had eaten Thanksgiving dinner on a troop train between Salt Lake City and Ardmore. This sure had been a busy year.

On November 22, we got our orders sending us back across the Atlantic to the good old USA, and on November 30th, we were sent to South Hampton to make the final leg of our journey home. We boarded the ship after dark, and were assigned a room about 10' by 10' with triple-decker bunks fastened to the walls. Chuck and I were the sole occupants. We were on the USS *George Washington*, a ship that the Merchant Marine took from Germany after World War I. We were issued life jackets and had to wear them every time we were out of the room. The German U-boat menace was still very real.

We awoke next morning and were pleasantly surprised by the breakfast. There were linen napkins and tablecloths, and food we hadn't seen since we left Goose Bay eight months ago. We moseyed out on deck and came upon an unbelievable scene. It seems someone looked down at some dockworkers, and decided to throw his British coins down to them. This attracted a crowd on the dock and another crowd up on the deck. Everybody up there started unloading their coins and the men below warmly welcomed them.

We pulled away from the dock at noon and soon found out we were in a convoy of thirty ships, and couldn't go any faster than the slowest ship. Our ship had been bringing troops over for a year or two, bringing six thousand at a time, hence the nine officers to a room. The enlisted men certainly were more crowded than this. There were two thousand of us going home, some like me, Air Corps men who had completed their missions, and some Navy men who had been on the D-Day landings. The rest were wounded men who were on their way back to hospitals at home. Most were on cots in a big area down below and most looked pretty bad. We were assigned hours to walk among them and make sure they didn't smoke. If we found any cigarettes, we had to take them away. Those poor guys hated our guts. The military had encouraged smoking, by giving them away or selling them cheaply, and now that they were hooked, they couldn't have one. There was nothing to help us pass the time. We could either look at the ocean, or go below and patrol the sick boys.

It was December, and on the cool side but the sea was calm. One of the crew told me, this was the smoothest crossing in December he had ever made. Seasickness didn't seem to be a problem; however one morning I went down for breakfast, and there on the white tablecloth, was a glass of grape juice at each plate. I took one look at that purple stuff and turned green. I got out on deck and after several deep breaths, I got my stomach under control and by lunchtime, I was back at the table.

I think we had destroyers with us the first part of the crossing, but I know on the latter part we had Canadian Corvettes scooting around us.

The next to last day, the weather warmed up, and most everyone took off his shirt to get some sun. Nobody got sunburned in England. The Air Corps navigators aboard were frustrated by their lack of equipment to determine our location so they could estimate our ETA. Everyone guessed that we were near Bermuda on the warm day.

The last day at sea was cold. In the middle of the afternoon after thirteen days, at sea we sailed into New York Harbor. We were welcomed by an army band, but by no happy families. Troop movements were big secrets, and no one was supposed to know about dockings. We grabbed our gear, and after a short ride, found ourselves at Fort Dix, NJ. That evening, our dinner was a big, fat steak with a fried egg on top. I don't even remember saying goodbye to Chuck, and then the next day, I was put on a train to Fort Meade, Maryland, and Chuck went a different direction.

Next morning at Ft. Meade, two other first lieutenants and I decided we needed to replenish some toilet articles and headed for the PX. As we were going in the door, a lieutenant Colonel came out, and we all said, "Hiya, Colonel." He must have thought he was hit by lightning, and came back inside, caught up with us and said, "Men, you're back in the States now and you don't just say "Hiya" to colonels, you salute them. So we gave them our best, rusty salute and the incident was over. He was nice about it, but he certainly was shook up about it.

Late that afternoon, I was sent to Washington, DC, and it must have been in the middle of the night when I boarded the train for Staunton, VA. I arrived in Staunton about six o'clock on the very cold morning of December 15. I walked a short distance to where US route 11 passes under the railroad, planning to hitchhike the 35 miles home. There were two half frozen GIs there going to Roanoke. They invited me to join them and shortly, a bread truck heading our way, picked us up and dropped me off at home.

Tattoos

Speaking of Anglo-American relationships, there was a story going around of four or five GIs going into a pub one evening. There, sitting at the bar was a British sailor drinking beer. He had imbibed more than he should have, and started making loud, derogatory remarks about the Yanks. He continued to drink, and continued his loud condemnation of the Americans. The GIs thought it was about time they take him outside and teach him some respect. The ranking GI said no, he had a better idea. He explained it and they all agreed. They began to buy him stronger drinks, and shortly thereafter, he passed out. They picked him up, carried him down the street to an emporium, and told the proprietor what they wanted and the proprietor agreed to it. They paid him and left. When the sailor came to, he looked down at his bare chest, and there in brilliant red, white, and blue colors, were tattooed the words "GOD BLESS AMERICA."

Stateside

CHAPTER 12

Bombardier Instructor School

15 December 1944 - 2 September 1945

It was good to be at home in Lexington, Virginia, for more than just a quick visit. My leave was for thirty days. I was to report on 15 January to the Richmond, Virginia, Army Air Corps Base (now Byrd Field) for further assignment.

I was glad I had stayed in England for those extra four months instead of coming home in September. It gave me time to catch my breath and resume a more normal schedule. I ate regularly, and gained back the weight I had lost flying the missions.

I know my family was glad to see me come home. A big load of worry had been lifted from my parents. My future seemed bright.

War time rationing was still in effect and Santa Claus had to be frugal for Christmas 1944. I went to the ration board and registered. I attended a holiday party and was able to contribute my two bottles of rationed liquor.

My dad had not visited his mother, who lived in Pennsylvania, since the war began. It seemed like a good time to visit. My dad, brother Ron and I took the train from Buena Vista, Virginia, to Sunbury, Pennsylvania, and arrived there at midnight in frigid weather. We were greeted by his mother, sister Anna, and her husband, Clarence Barrow. A day or two later we drove to Lancaster, Pennsylvania, to visit his brother Herman. My uncle Herman had been a Seaman in WW I, and was a staunch member of the American Legion. He took me to an American Legion meeting and had a ball showing me off.

My grandparents were both born in Berlin, Germany. My grandfather had died in 1940. During the war, Grandmother was torn between being a loyal American, and concern for her kin in Germany. She refused to believe the stories of Nazi atrocities, and concentration camps; she thought they were all lies. I had to soft pedal my recent flights over the Fatherland.

We took a quick trip to Williamsport, Pennsylvania, to visit my mother's brother Laird and his sons Jay and Bill. After we returned home, we also made a couple of day visits to Covington, Virginia, where we had lived for six years, and where I had graduated from high school. All my school friends were still in service or scattered to the four corners of the globe.

The thirty-days leave went by in a flash. On 15 January 1945 I presented myself at the base in Richmond. I was to report for Roll Call at 8:00 a.m. but had the rest of the day for myself. I met a returned pilot from Meherrin, Virginia, who said he was going home over the weekend, and invited me to go along. I accepted and spent two nights at his parents' home. He had a girl friend at Farmville State Teachers College (now Longwood College), so we headed there. His date knew a girl from Covington, who was a year or two behind me in school and the four of us spent a pleasant evening together.

Rather than spend weekends in Richmond, I went home each Friday. I eventually found a phone number for the base, where I could find out if my name was on shipping orders. One Sunday I called, and found out I had to be at the base at 8:00 a.m. Monday. I rode a late night bus to Richmond, fell asleep, and when I woke up I was in the car barn, all by myself. Next morning I received my new assignment.

When I had first arrived in Richmond they asked to what part of the country I wished to be sent. I told them, anywhere east of the Mississippi. In true army custom, I found myself heading for Midland, Texas. I went by rail, in some sort of traveling Rail Barracks Troop Train. The cars had been equipped with double deck bunks on each side of the center aisle with some open space furnished with easy chairs at the end. These cars were attached to a regular train. We ate all our meals in the dining car with the civilian passengers.

Midland was a nice place, reportedly a hotbed of oil millionaires, and the air base was just outside of town. It had been a bombardier school for aviation cadets for a couple of years, and now, a portion was set aside to train bombardier instructors. I almost felt I was back in cadets, as we were housed in the same barracks as the cadets.

In order to draw flying pay, one had to fly a minimum of four hours a month. If three months were missed, flight pay was lost. None of us had flown since we left England, so a flight was arranged, and we were jammed into an old Army version of the DC-3, and circled the base for four hours.

We ate in the officers mess, but the food was not as good as Santa Ana and Victorville. We met with some frustration in the Midland base mess hall. The commanding officer was a full colonel and a West Pointer. He had never been overseas and was apparently jealous of men who had seen combat, and was trying to downplay our experiences. He had a wall built in front of the serving line. To eat, one had to walk along this wall, where one could not see the food. At the end of this line, one made a U-turn to get his meal. There was a little niche where he stood, in order to inspect the uniforms. If every thing wasn't to his liking, he took you out of line and sent you back to your barracks to correct it. He especially looked for any over-seas patches or insignia. You were ordered to remove these and replace them with training command insignia. This certainly irked us to put it mildly.

The training was similar to Victorville. We flew the same AT-11 training planes, dropped the same 100-pound bombs, and even the desert looked the same. The only difference was a "glide bomb" attachment to the Norden bombsight. Glide bombing was a compromise between level bombing and dive bombing. I have often wondered if any glide bombing ever occurred in combat. If so, I have not heard of it.

On one of our training flights, the bail-out horn started honking, and one of the engines quit. I put on my parachute and looked down on that bleak West Texas landscape and said to myself, "I sure do not want to jump out into that desert. I'll probably land on a rattlesnake or a tarantula." The pilot was frantically hitting switches, pushing, and pulling things. The engine finally coughed, and came to life. He had forgotten to transfer fuel from one tank to another and it went dry. That pilot had probably just gotten his wings the previous week. He learned a good lesson that day.

After nine weeks at Midland, I received a diploma on 4 April 1945, and was sent to the air base at Childress, Texas, as a bombardier instructor.

Why the Air Corps sent me to Childress, Texas, is something neither I, the training command nor the Pentagon could explain. There were no bombers here, and I am not sure there were even any kind of airplanes on the base. I was rooming with Don Mickle, another bombardier who had returned from combat. He was a 1st lieutenant also. We had absolutely nothing to do except to eat and sleep. Our room had wooden walls, floors, and ceiling. It was furnished with two cots and a window. We were so bored we decided to decorate the place. We started by getting a hammer and some nails. We hammered nails into the walls to hang things on, and then went into town to search the used furniture stores. Our first acquisition was a pair of unmatched easy chairs. After we got tired of these, we went back to town and bought a round wooden table, which cost us $5.00. In both cases, we had to pay a dollar or two to have our purchases delivered to the base. Just as we were beginning to feel at home, we were shipped out.

5 May 1945 - Pyote, Texas

We left for the 236th Army Air Base Bombardment Unit. It was a long, hot trip on a civilian bus. There was a raspy radio on the bus, and when it blared out the wonderful news of the German surrender, we were really excited. It made the trip bearable.

The nickname for Pyote was "Rattlesnake Tower." Rumor had it that 5,000 rattlers were killed while grading the property for the runways and buildings. It was located along US Rt. 90, between Odessa and El Paso, twenty miles east of Pecos, Texas.

Outside the base was a post office, a filling station, and a couple of nondescript houses. I talked with a resident who said he was born in Virginia, but all he could recall was how green it was. Here, he said, you could look farther and see less than any place in the world.

I was pleased that I would be flying in B-29s. I had heard a lot about them, but having never been near one, thought it was the biggest plane I had ever seen, and the most beautiful. It was built by the Boeing Company, who had also built the B-17. The two had little in common. The B-17 had two men in the nose, the B-29 had six, (bombardier, two pilots, a flight engineer, a navigator, and a radio operator). There were seats for each man, since the nose space was approximately 8" x 10." It seemed like a theater balcony where one was able to look down and watch the scenery passing underneath.

The crew areas could be pressurized, which meant no oxygen masks were needed until the plane went into combat and then the cabin became depressurized.

There were two bomb bays behind the nose and the waist gunner area was behind turrets, each containing two 50-caliber machine guns. The firing system was state of the art, electronically controlled; control was automatically passed between the bombardier and the three waist gunners. Each of the men had an electronic gun sight, and each gunner had a Plexiglas "blister" to shoot from, one on top the plane, and one on each side.

The tail gunner was isolated from the rest of the crew, and there was no passageway between him and the rest of the plane. He entered his station via a ladder from the ground. When the plane was in flight there was no access to him in case of an emergency. There was a tunnel, between the nose and the waist, but its diameter was minimal, and even I had trouble navigating the twenty-five- or thirty-foot length.

On paper, the B-29 looked a dream, but the plane had many problems. There was a good bit of aluminum in those four 2,000-horsepower engines, and they had a bad habit of catching fire. A flight mechanic once told me he thought each plane had been built by a team, and not on an assembly line. The wiring had not been standardized. Each plane had been wired differently and when a problem originated, the mechanic was forced to start from scratch, and trace every line from beginning to end.

The B-29s were difficult to fly, and I have read that more B-29 crews were killed in training accidents than in combat missions.

My instructor duties were very vague, but I was assigned to report to the flight line every morning. Actually, I flew once or twice every week, but never was there another bombardier to be instructed, so I just sat there in the nose and looked out at that gosh awful scenery. Our flights lasted about seven hours, and figuring in pre-flight and post-flight time, it turned out to be a ten-hour day.

After the novelty of this plane wore off I got pretty bored. The others in the nose were busy with their duties so I would go through the tunnel, back to the waist, and talk with the three bored gunners. We discussed the firing system from the waist, but I never had any instruction about shooting from the nose position.

The living accommodations at Pyote were spartan. The barracks was constructed of wood, 100 percent. It was about 100 feet long with a hall down one long side, and two dozen partitioned cubicles down the other. Our room was about 8' x 8' with one window but no door. The partitions were a foot off the floor and a foot down from the ceiling. A cooling system of a sort, resembling a wooden chimney was located along the wall. It was filled with Spanish moss, and at one time must have had water flowing through it, but it was no longer operational. The rooms were stinking hot during the day, but cooled off nicely when the sun went down. I can't picture the mess hall, and I can't remember the food so I guess it was like most Army food, neither real good, nor real bad.

Two species of wild life were abundant here, horned toads and tarantulas. The toads were easy to catch and they didn't mind being picked up. The tarantulas looked dangerous, but you could pick one up. It would crawl all over you. If they were on the ground and you moved one with your foot, it would jump two feet high.

One morning I went out to the latrine, and there under a sink, stretched out, was a three-foot rattlesnake. I yelled for someone to bring me a stick, and in a minute someone showed up with a broom, and gave it a couple of good whacks. Good-bye snake.

A nice break in the routine occurred when one of the guys in the barracks, who owned a car, invited three of us to Carlsbad, New Mexico, to visit the caverns. We left the next morning, a Saturday, arriving there about noon, and secured rooms. The place was polluted with khaki uniforms, and we wandered around all afternoon. Later after we found an evening meal, we went to the movies, and saw Elizabeth Taylor and Mickey Rooney in *National Velvet*. That was one exciting day.

The next morning, we were up bright and early and headed for the caverns. A United States Park Service ranger gave the talk, and we followed him down underground. It was an awe-inspiring piece of geology, and something I have never forgotten. We walked down for six hours, taking short stops along the way. The guide at one stop asked if we would like to see it just as Mother Nature made it before the Park Service built all the trails and added other improvements. Of course, we all said yes, and he hit a switch. I never experienced such darkness as surrounded us there. We kept walking until we reached our destination, the lunch counter.

After we ate, the elevator took us up to the surface. The temperature inside the Cavern was 52 degrees, when we stepped out of the elevator; the temperature was over a hundred. It felt like being hit with a baseball bat. There were several Indians at the surface selling hand made silver jewelry. I have often wished I had purchased something.

For my three years in the Army, I cannot recall ever getting a hair cut until I got to Pyote. The only reason I remember that is because the main barber always attempted to sell hair tonic, too. His sales pitch was, "What are you doing for your hair in this dry desert air?" Perhaps if I had bought a bottle, today I would have a better head of hair.

Another happy weekend occurred when I got a message from Chuck Baker. He and Donnabeth were now happily married, and stationed at San Angelo, not too far from Pyote. He was training pilots in instrument flying, using AT-6s. This was a neat, two seat plane, with a 650-hp engine, retractable wheels, radio, and plenty of instruments. Later they were used to portray Jap Zeroes in war movies and were painted white, with a big red "meat ball" on the wings and side.

Chuck said he would fly to Pyote, pick me up, and fly us back to San Angelo for the week-end. He arrived as planned, I buckled my seat belt and sat back anticipating a leisurely ride. He rammed the throttle forward, and told me to take it off. The torque of that big engine was more than I had expected, and before I knew it, I was over a hanger, rather than the runway. The remainder of the ride was equally exciting. He showed me every acrobatic maneuver in the book. I was blacked out half the time, and the other half I spent tightening my seat belt. We flew down a narrow river, and as I looked back, I could see the water returning to where we had blown it out.

I had a great time with them and got to know Donnabeth, and enjoyed her good cooking. I returned to Pyote by bus, never realizing I would not see the Bakers again until 1983, thirty-eight years later.

I was getting pretty restless at Pyote, I did not have enough to do, only flying once or twice a week. The rest of the time, I loafed around the officers club. It was nice and had a swimming pool which I used every afternoon. I went to the movies every night after supper, and then hit the sack. Everyone here seemed bored. I believe there was more hard liquor consumed than water at this base.

I missed my old crew. Don Mickle, who came here with me from Childress, had moved off base with his wife and young daughter into a two-room apartment. Actually, it was one room with a curtain stretched across the middle.

I didn't have any close pals, and ideas of leaving Pyote invaded my thinking.

We had a class about ready to move on, and I thought I could be put on one of those crews. Or at least I could volunteer to go to the Pacific. All this became moot, when on 6

August 1945, the B-29 Enola Gay, dropped an Atomic Bomb on Hiroshima, Japan. A couple of days later a second one was dropped on Nagasaki, Japan. The bombardier who dropped the second bomb was Captain Kermit Beehan, who had been head of the bombardier section back at Ardmore.

14 August 1945 the Japanese government surrendered, and World War II came to a close.

It took a few days for us to realize the war was really over, but when the base commander declared a 48-hour period of rejoicing, I then decided it was for real. All gates around the base were locked, and no one could come or go. Every thing was shut down, except the service clubs, the theatre, the mess halls, and the PX. It became the wildest, most drunken party ever seen. Cases of booze were brought out, and placed on the tables of the officers club for all to enjoy. Guys were jumping into the swimming pool fully clothed, acting like wild men. The crews realized they probably would not be going overseas, and they couldn't contain themselves. I decided to join in the festivities, and drank more than I had any reason to. I woke up in the middle of the night, sick as a dog, and threw up everything I had eaten in the past week. One poor celebrator awoke in the furnace room of the base chapel, stark naked. He had passed out, and someone had dragged him in there, took his wallet, shoes and every strip of his clothes.

By the end of the second day, every one was worn out, and things slowly returned to normal. But it took a while.

Now, the only topic of conversation was of getting out, and returning to civilian life. Everyone had a different idea of how it should be accomplished. One soldier wrote a letter to the editor of the *Yank* magazine, saying the only fair way would be alphabetically. He signed his letter A. A. Aaron.

It was finally announced, discharges would be calculated on a "points" system.

There would be one for every month of service, one for every month overseas. One also received five points, for every medal, or "Oak Leaf Cluster," or battle star. 50 points were needed for one to be considered for discharge. I counted my points, and came up with 85. I applied and didn't have to wait very long for my discharge to come through.

The period between my arrival back in the States and this ending of my time at Pyote, was the most unrewarding of my military experience. It had all been "make do" something to keep me occupied while waiting for something else. After all my new and exciting experiences including pre-flight school, soloing an airplane, mastering the Norden Bombsight, the pioneer flight across the Atlantic, England, the missions, with something new every day, duty at Pyote was the "pits" by comparison.

One of the guys in my barracks was a pilot from Bristol, Virginia. Fred had a wife living off base and he spent some nights with her but when he was scheduled to fly, he slept on base. He had a pre-war Ford, which reminded me of *Sequatchee*: ready for a museum, or the junk yard. Our orders to head east were dated the same day, and after some discussion, he agreed to take me along. At noon on a Monday, the three of us and all our worldly possessions, jammed into that car, said goodbye to Pyote, heading for Bristol.

By noon on Tuesday, we were driving into Arkansas, halfway to our destination. We stopped only for gas, food, and rest rooms. Interstate highways were a thing of the future, and our route took us right down the main street of every city, town, and village, stopping for every traffic light. At noon the second day, after 48 hours on the road, that Ford pulled into the yard of Fred's home. His parents were quite hospitable, and invited me to stay with them, and I asked, "Where is the bed?" I stayed with them a couple of days, running around with Fred and wife visiting all their kinfolk. There surely were a lot of them.

21 September 1945, Fred and I got back in the Ford, and drove to Fort Bragg, North Carolina, near Raleigh. This was a separation center where we were formally released from U.S. military service. We were given a physical exam, which took about five minutes. They didn't want to find anything which would require the government to pay for in the future. They talked me into joining the Air Corps Reserve, gave me my final pay, with $300.00 discharge bonus. With that, I was promoted from 1st Lt. Ordel to Civilian Ordel. Fred drove me back to South Boston, Virginia, where I boarded a bus home to Lexington.

It is impossible for me to measure the impact of those three years in the Army Air Corps on my life. It was unique, it was exciting, it was an emotional roller coaster, it was educational, it was challenging, it was humbling, it was scary, it was boring, there was glory, and there were disappointments. There was sadness, there was glee, and it was indescribable. Every day brought something new, and even the most incredible events seemed routine. What a life!

Postscript

Where are the presidents? This is me in front of the White House on the morning of the ceremony.

It's getting closer. Awaiting the ceremony with the other honorees

And Closer. Talking with the president of France, Francois Hollande.

The Deed is Done. Being pinned by the French president.

Keswick man among veterans
honored by French president

Sen. Tim Kaine meets with World War II veteran George Shepolo next to Robert Selm (in far).
during a reception at the Fort Myer Officer's Club in Arlington on Tuesday.

French Legion Of Honor Medal

Our own Art Ordel spent a whirlwind two days in Washington, D.C., and Fort Myer, Virginia, on February 10th and 11th as one of six World War Two veterans being honored by France for their help in liberating the French from the Nazi German occupation during World War Two. The six veterans each received the Knights Badge of the French Legion of Honor at an afternoon ceremony on Tuesday, February 11, 2014. The French President Francois Hollande was in the United States on a three-day state visit and presented the medal to each recipient.

Art's day, on Tuesday, February 11, began with breakfast at the White House, followed at midday by a luncheon at the State Department, and late afternoon by the award ceremony at Fort Myer, near Arlington National Cemetery. Following the award ceremony there were champagne and French pastries. Before his arrival at the award ceremony, French President Hollande made a similar award of the French Legion of Honor to the Unknown Soldier buried in the Arlington National Cemetery.

Art was awarded the Distinguished Flying Cross and the Air Medal with four Oak Leaf Clusters for flying 35 missions during the war, with sixteen of the missions being over France.

A reception and dinner honoring Art's service, given by the local American Legion Post 74, was held on Thursday, February 20, after the originally scheduled event of February 13, was postponed due to snow. A large number of Art's family members, many friends, and fellow Legion members attended this reception. Art received many commendations from state and local groups and individuals, including the honoring of Art by the local Monticello District of the Stonewall Jackson Council of Boy Scouts with a summer camp fellowship in Art's name to go each year to a deserving scout member.